Systems Trading for Spread Betting

An end-to-end guide for developing
spread betting systems

Gary Ford

HARRIMAN HOUSE LTD

3A Penns Road
Petersfield
Hampshire
GU32 2EW
GREAT BRITAIN

Tel: +44 (0)1730 233870
Fax: +44 (0)1730 233880
Email: enquiries@harriman-house.com
Website: www.harriman-house.com

First published in Great Britain in 2008 by Harriman House.

Copyright © Harriman House Ltd

The right of Gary Ford to be identified as the author has been asserted
in accordance with the Copyright, Design and Patents Act 1988.

ISBN 978-1-905641-73-4

British Library Cataloguing in Publication Data
A CIP catalogue record for this book can be obtained from the British Library.

Printed by the MPG Books Group in the UK.

Contents

Acknowledgments

I'd like to thank my family, friends and pets for being patient with me during the time I spent writing this book. I would also like to thank Tom Hougaard (www.tradertom.com), Ian Bowman, Huw Griffiths and Paul Elson for their ever positive feedback, Dave "Casper" Gale for keeping me interested in computing, NinjaTrader for developing great software, and the team at Harriman House for giving me this opportunity.

Gary Ford

May 2008

Preface

What the book covers

My aim for this book is to provide a practical guide that will detail all of the steps I use when developing, testing and executing a trading system specifically for spread betting. The steps are based around a series of hands-on examples of turning a strategy into a trading system. The book contains the steps I have used and the avenues, benefits, pitfalls, tips and tricks that I have discovered during my development of systems trading strategies. The book is not a guide on how to trade, and does not dwell on styles of trading. It is purely a description of what I did, what I found to be successful and what I found did not work well. I appreciate that everyone has different trading styles, and hence I will try and approach the book with an unbiased view.

This book is also not about market behaviour, trader psychology, and details on how to spread bet, or a book of off-the-shelf strategies that you could use for spread betting. Throughout this book I have used a free strategy development system called NinjaTrader. Whilst many of the examples given show detailed steps on how to create them with NinjaTrader, this book should not be considered a user manual for NinjaTrader. To learn how to use NinjaTrader the reader should take a look at the www.ninjatrader.com website and take part in many of the fantastic free seminars that the NinjaTrader team organise each week.

Some of the strategies developed in this book have been successful and some have not been profitable. My intention behind this book is not to give you a strategy to go and trade, but to give you the knowledge and methodology to use the tools to develop many successful strategies of your own.

Malcolm Pryor's book, *The Financial Spread Betting Handbook*, covers the end-to-end process of spread betting in detail, and should be considered a great reference for those wishing to understand more about spread betting.

Who this is for

This book will be suited to the intermediate level spread bettor who currently has at least one trading strategy, and is looking to develop that strategy into a system strategy to reduce the amount of manual intervention needed. In addition, this book will help the intermediate spread bettor to enhance/prove the performance of their strategy by developing it into a trading system and backtesting it against historical data.

How the book is structured

The book is structured to follow the steps needed for the trader to progress from being an intermediate-level spread bettor through to having a developed, tested and working system trading strategy for spread betting.

Introduction

'The stock market is a dangerous place to be, be sure to stay away' was the advice given by my peers. And after years of investing in instruments such as government bonds, high interest savings accounts and cash ISAs I had turned a moderate pile of cash into a slightly larger pile of cash. No emotion. No research. Just straightforward, and rather dull, investing. Or to be more accurate, someone else investing my money for me. Whilst the returns were fairly moderate, they were acceptable to me.

I then progressed onto the next rung of the investing ladder by subscribing to a weekly finance magazine. Each week, several highly qualified investment gurus would list all of their top stock-picks for the weeks, months and years ahead. Obviously these gurus knew their stuff, so I blindly purchased their recommendations. Fortunately for me a steadily growing bull market carried my purchases along nicely – and still today, even with a few of the recent wobbles, my investment portfolio is happily earning dividends, but it is never going to earn me a living or allow me to achieve financial freedom.

After a few more years, and more hot-tip subscriptions, my buy and hold strategy became as boring as my initial reaction to government bonds. With broadband at home and a constant connection to all of the information on the Internet, I finally did some research into the black art of trading. Spread betting to be more accurate. After the initial excitement of trading a "player account" for a few months, I naturally progressed into opening a full account and funding it with real money! After attending several free seminars – surrounded by other gamblers and reading many books on trading, I had a good understanding about technical analysis, and why I needed to use it. As they say, a little knowledge is dangerous. After several months of good fun on the highly emotional trading rollercoaster my account was back to just above its initial starting point. Whilst I wanted to continue with my discretionary trading, both my day job and my lack of trading experience were getting in my way. Sensibly, I chose not to give up the day job, but to spend my spare time researching trading.

Many more years, books and courses followed. Many trades on both the player account and live account were logged and analysed, with simple trading strategies providing small but consistent returns. The emotional roller coaster still existed, but felt like it was under control. I still had the urge to give up the day job, until I discovered system trading. As I had spent the best part of 11 years in the IT industry, I was very familiar with the use of automation. System trading appeared to offer the holy grail of trading. I could code up my trading strategies and get them to notify me of buy and sell signals. All of the automation would run in the background without much, if any, input from me. The trades would be clear cut, based on tested strategies, with no emotion involved. I could do this and still keep the day job!

This book details my journey in the world of system trading for spread betting. It is important to understand that every trader has his or her own approach, and that it is very easy to trade someone else's profitable strategy and still make a loss because the strategy cannot be moulded to the trader. I believe that it is very important to develop and refine a strategy to match your lifestyle. Doing so will ensure that you do not deviate from the strategy. I have made many mistakes during this journey, and learnt a lot about myself in the process. I have also learnt many tricks and shortcuts which have made my trading easier to manage and more profitable. I hope to share them with you throughout the course of this book.

Trading Systems

Discretionary Traders

A discretionary trader uses a combination of intuition, advice and technical or fundamental data to determine when to enter and exit a trade. Because this trading methodology employs no quantifiable game plan, the discretionary trader tries to predict the market, but no one knows for certain where the market is going, when it will move, or which market will be the next big mover. The discretionary trader does not always make the same interpretation of a market indicator, or use it in the same fashion every time. The trader uses his or her own judgement to predict the market move. I am not suggesting that the discretionary trader does not have a strategy, as all successful traders require a strategy to enable them to have an edge over the market. The use of personal judgement gives the discretionary trader the advantage of flexibility of whether to take the trade or not, but of course this judgement can fall foul of human emotion. Also, because of the manual effort involved in performing the analysis, much more time and effort must be exerted during trading. An advantage of discretionary trading is that the trader develops their intuition about the market or instruments they are trading.

Trading Strategies

Strategies are all about probability. When creating a strategy we aim to create one that has a higher probability of profit than loss. Trading success comes from high probabilities and not certainty. It is impossible to eliminate losses, so we aim to minimise them.

Put simply, a trading strategy is a predefined set of rules to be met before opening, managing and closing a trade. Strategies range from the straightforward crossing over of moving averages through to multiple indicator, multiple time frame analysis with pattern recognition and artificial intelligence.

The purpose of the strategy is to give the trader – or their computer – the pre-defined set of rules to follow each and every time a trade is to be placed or exited. Creating and following a strategy can give a trader the edge they need to be successful in the markets.

Trading Systems

A popular belief is that human emotion, specifically greed and fear, are some of the greatest barriers to becoming a successful trader. Most readers will be familiar with the phrase "cut your losses, and let your profits run". Just as many readers will have encountered a series of sequential losing trades and have stalled instead of placing the next trade, or held on to a losing trade instead of closing out the losing position, and instead end up watching the position go further and further away.

A **trading system** wraps trading formulas into an order and execution system. Advanced computer modeling techniques, combined with electronic access to world market data and information, enable traders using a trading system to have a unique market vantage point. Traders, investment firms and fund managers use a trading system to help make wiser investment decisions and help eliminate the emotional aspect of trading. A trading system can automate all or part of your investment portfolio. Computer trading models can be adjusted for either conservative or aggressive trading styles.

A trading system is governed by a set of rules that do not deviate based on anything other than market action. Emotional bias is eliminated because the systems operate within the parameters known by the trader. The parameters can be trusted based on historical analysis and real world market studies, so that the trader who is familiar with the trading system and its operating characteristics can have confidence in a pre-determined trading strategy.

The three elements that make up a trading system are:

1. The strategy formula itself. Benefiting from a successful testing phase, and expected to provide profitable returns.

2. A money management strategy. Often this is closely interwoven with the strategy formula, as poor money management of a winning formula can still empty an account.

3. Trader discipline. The systems trader needs to have the discipline to trade the signals generated by the strategy, unless the strategy is fully automated and the positions are controlled automatically.

Misconceptions Of Trading Systems

I recently attended a seminar in London about mechanical trading systems. Whilst talking about system performance analysis, the seminar presenter discussed that he would not trade a system that had less than an 80% success rate. This is a figure that I think would be hard to find in the majority of mechanical strategies.

Trading systems are not the holy grail of trading. A trading system is likely to have just as many losing trades as discretionary trading strategies.

My personal views on mechanical systems are as follows:

• They have been developed in such a way so as to be generalised enough to be profitable for a range of instruments.

• They are robust enough to withstand a variety of market conditions, or have rules in place to know when to stop trading if unfavourable conditions appear.

• They will compute in the background, taking trades that meet a certain criteria without the need for constant human analysis.

High Level System Descriptions

Aggressive

An aggressive system would be one that typically exhibits some or all of the following characteristics:

- Larger drawdowns. Perhaps through not having stop-loss levels set, or through having very wide stops.

- Holds open positions longer. Holding onto a losing position usually results in a larger drawdown. The system is hoping for a change in market direction to take the trade back into profit. Conversely, the system is also prepared to hold onto a winning position longer in the hope that further gains can be achieved.

- Higher number of open trades. These can be open positions of the same instrument at different prices and stakes, or multiple positions in different instruments.

- Sporadic equity curve. Likely due to taking on large position sizes.

- Curve fitted. The system has been over optimised and only appears to generate gains for a specific instrument and a particular market condition. These systems typically have a very short lifetime or fail from the outset.

- More frequent trades.

- Less restrictive entry criteria/filters.

- Higher percentage of capital risked per trade.

Cautious

A cautious trading system would typically exhibit some of the following characteristics:

- Low frequency of trades due to more restrictive trade entry criteria.

- Large emphasis on capital preservation, so a smaller amount of capital risked per trade.

- Wider range of instruments traded to provide an average return over multiple markets.

Moderate

A moderate trading system exhibits traits of both the aggressive and cautious trading systems, with perhaps an in-depth focus on market conditions to decide when to take on more risk.

Other Definitions Used Throughout This Book

Spread Betting Company is the commonly used term to identify the majority of companies that offer financial spread betting. In financial commerce the term **broker** is used to identify an intermediary who acts between a buyer and seller. Technically a pure spread betting company is more of a bookmaker than a broker as they take the other side of your trades. However, in order to make this book more readable, I shall use the terms broker and spread betting companies interchangeably throughout.

I have also used the term **instrument** to cover the whole range of equities, futures, currencies, indices, etc. that can be traded through spread betting. Throughout this book the trading focus is on currencies/foreign exchange, yet the term instrument rather than currency pair is still used because much of the content of this book is applicable to all things tradable. The term instrument also matches the term used in the strategy development software used throughout this book.

Other terms and definitions can be found in the glossary at the back of this book.

Reasons To Trade

Psychology is an important aspect of trading. Even with system trading, psychology still plays an active role. There exist many great books on trading psychology, and hence I will not be covering this topic in any depth. However I do feel that it is important to address why we are trading.

Why are we trading?

Everyone has a different reason to trade, some of the common reasons include:

- Income. Trading to live.

- Career change.

- Excitement. Living to trade.

- Boasting rights, or trying to impress.

- Boredom and looking for a challenge.

- Additional funds each month to supplement the day job.

- Creation of a portfolio of trading strategies to replicate a mini hedge fund.

Realistic goals

As with discretionary trading, system trading also relies on the trader having realistic expectations. Whilst I have regularly used strategies that have increased my account capital by 20% in a day, I have also seen those profits disappear on other days. If you aim to double your capital every few months, and you have a strategy to do this that you are happy with, then this is a realistic goal. However, personally my realistic goals involve having a series of low to medium risk strategies that generate a return that outperforms general investments such as cash, bonds or index trackers, coupled with the tax-free status of spread betting.

Different ways to use a trading system

There exist many ways to trade a trading system, but the three most popular ways include:

- Follow all of the buy and sell signals religiously. This involves great discipline and faith that the trading system is profitable. Following this method should ensure that the performance results resemble the results seen during testing.

- Use the systems signals as guidance. In Jack Schwager's book, *New Market Wizards*, many of the successful traders mention that they use trading systems to generate buy and sell signals, and then apply their own market knowledge to the signal to decide whether to proceed with the trade.

- Use the system to open the trade, but use discretionary principles to manage and exit the trade.

Conclusion

We can conclude from this introductory chapter that by using trading systems for spread betting we can achieve many things, including:

- Allowing a computer application to generate trading signals based on our current strategies, thus removing some of the repetitive effort from our trading and leaving the trader with more time to spend on further analysis, system development, or just time to relax.

- By developing our strategies into trading systems we can backtest them against a range of time frames, instruments and historic data to see how our strategies would have performed under various market conditions.

Throughout the remainder of this book we will analyse, develop, backtest and optimise several example trading systems.

2

Why Choose Spread Betting?

Brief Overview Of Financial Spread Betting

In the UK, financial spread betting is a form of derivative gambling that allows a trader to take a position based on the expected price of an instrument or index without actually owning the underlying asset. Whilst technically classed as gambling, it differs from conventional fixed odds betting – such as sports betting – as the profits or losses sustained fluctuate continually until the position is closed. For example, with a fixed odds bet, the maximum losses are the entire value of the stake, but with spread betting the theoretical maximum losses are unlimited.

Benefits Of Spread Betting

Tax-free

At the time of writing spread betting in the UK is classed as gambling, and the proceeds of gambling are classed as tax-free unless Her Majesty's Revenue and Customs (HMRC) determine that you are a professional gambler, which is a remarkably grey area. Simply studying many of the contradicting examples on the HMRC website does not make this any clearer, but I believe we can say that currently spread betting is tax-free as the act of placing a spread bet is not normally associated with carrying on a profession. It is generally believed that gambling is tax-free so that the gambling public do not receive tax relief on their losses. This also shows that even the government believe that more people make losses from spread betting than make profits! The generally quoted figure is that 85% of spread bettors are unsuccessful.

As the profits of a spread bet are tax-free, also the placing of a spread bet is tax-free. Typically if you were to purchase UK listed shares you would pay stamp duty, currently at 0.5%.

Zero commission

With traditional purchasing of shares, a fee or commission is paid to the broker every time a position is opened or closed. The fee varies depending on the broker used, but at the time of writing a typical fee for a broker dealing with retail clients is in the order of £20-30 per round turn, ie, the total cost to the trader to open and close a trade.

No commission is charged when opening or closing a position using spread betting, but the spreads are sufficiently wide enough for the spread betting company to make a profit, which could potentially be classed as a commission.

Large choice of instruments

Financial spread bettors can place trades on a large number of instruments, including, but not limited to:

- Equities
- Stock indices
- Currencies
- Commodities
- Interest rates
- Futures
- Options

Large choice of spread betting companies

There exists a large number of spread betting companies trading in the UK. Many companies offer incentives for you to open an account with them, and choosing which companies to trade with is a matter of personal preference. Some are better than others, but it is fair to say that they are in constant competition with each other, so the trading interface features, customer service and incentives are getting better all of the time.

Gearing

Financial gearing, leverage, or margin trading is the use of capital in such a way that the potential positive or negative outcome is magnified. Leverage is the proverbial double edged sword. It can lead to large profits from a small stake, and also (theoretically) unlimited losses that far exceed your initial deposit. If the latter happens, expect to receive a margin call from the spread betting company. A margin call happens when the account capital remaining in the traders account is insufficient to cover existing positions as the trades move against the trader.

Small account size

With the help of gearing, small position sizes and generous incentives from the spread betting companies, it is very easy to start trading with a small account in the order of only a few hundred pounds. However, the restrictions of a small account become apparent as soon as you start to trade. Your position size will be restricted, and you may find that you have to place your stops very tight, constantly running the risk of being stopped out with even the slightest market volatility. We cover account sizing in a later chapter.

Player accounts

Nearly every spread betting company offers a "player account" to allow customers to get used to using their trading platform or interface. Whilst the types of orders and trading mechanics are almost identical between companies, the interfaces to place those trades can vary greatly. Player accounts are great for getting up to speed with an interface without risking any capital. They are also very useful for risk-free real-time testing of a trading strategy.

Disadvantages Of Spread Betting

Large spreads

The spread in the term spread betting refers to the price difference between the bid and offer price quoted by the spread betting company. The bid and offer prices displayed by the company are different to the market prices for the same instrument because additional points are added around the live price. For example, if the FTSE 100 Cash price is currently 6540, then a spread betting company may quote a price of 6539 – 6541. Therefore the spread for this instrument would be two points.

The size of the spreads vary greatly depending on which spread betting company is used. Many companies offer tight spreads for the popular instruments. Some of the instruments on offer have such large spreads that, depending on your strategy, it is difficult to profit unless a large move occurs.

For example, if you are looking to day trade an instrument that has an average daily movement of only sixteen points, yet it has a spread of eight points, you could lose 50% of your potential profit to the spread. The trader should consider whether it is worth actually trading this instrument.

Prices are indicative only

The price quoted by the spread betting company is indicative of the actual price of the underlying instrument. Spread betting is not traded through an exchange. The price quoted is not the exact price because of the spread, and sometimes the price appears to be totally out of step with what the instrument is doing. The trader also has no way of investigating why their orders were filled or not filled, or how the underlying prices are actually created. For much of the time when I actually sit and watch my trades in progress, I regularly notice that the price and price movements I see in my charting package do not match the price and price movements quoted to me by the spread betting company. I believe that this may be because:

- It would be costly in terms of computing power for the spread betting company to quote prices on a tick-by-tick basis, so the price may only be updated once per second or less.

- The prices in my charting package, whilst being subscribed to a real-time data feed, must suffer with some latency from the actual exchange prices because of the latency factor, and the processing that is performed on them before they arrive at my PC. For example, if a UK based trader is using a US based data provider whilst trading the FTSE 100 Cash, the data provider must receive their data from the London Stock Exchange, which has been transferred across the Atlantic, processed and formatted by the data providers servers, and then returned back to the UK over the internet to my PC. I would expect this latency to be at least two seconds or more. (See side note below.)

- Over the counter products such as forex do not have a single exchange to provide data. The prices are usually quoted from multiple sources, so it is highly likely that the multiple sources have slightly different prices – possibly good for arbitrage – and also highly likely that your spread betting company and your charting software each get their data from different sources.

When discussing computer networks and data transmission, the time taken or delay before data arrives – in this case price data for real-time charts – is called latency. Latency is measured in milliseconds. An additional factor that delays the real-time data arriving in the traders charting package is processing delay. Processing delay occurs when the computers performing calculations on the real-time data need to output the data into a specific format. Latency from a UK based exchange to a US data provider, and then back to the UK could be summarised as:

- London to UK coast, delay 30ms

- 1st journey over the Atlantic Ocean to the US, delay 95ms

- US data provider processing, delay 1000ms

- 2nd journey over the Atlantic Ocean back to the UK, delay 95ms

- UK coast back to London, delay 30ms

- Trader charting package processing, delay 500ms

The total round trip latency for the real-time data is the summation of all of these delays. In this example the real-time data is actually 1.75 seconds old. Whilst this is a negligible value for most traders, it may have an affect if your trading strategy works on ultra-short timescales.

Being re-quoted and execution delays

Many spread bettors believe that the price seems to change more when they are near to closing a position. The same is true when opening a position. There appears to be an inherent delay from the time clicked on the buy button (for opening a trade) or the close button. This delay almost always results in the trade being opened or closed at a different price. Obviously the higher the volatility of the instrument, the higher the possible difference in price. Sometimes this does work in your favour and you get a few extra points, however – taking into account human psychology – the price often seems to take a few points away from you.

Limitations on order placement

Many professional trading applications allow all types of orders to be placed including; limit order, buy stop, sell stop, open if touched, the ability to reverse orders, and the automatic placement of stops and profit targets at the same time the order is filled.

Useful order types and position management tools are on offer with some spread betting companies, but they are not the norm. Although I have a cynical view with spread betting that, since you are betting against the company and not the market, giving them this information could allow them to manipulate your position. For example, by introducing a delay in the time it takes them to close your order when the profit target is reached.

The majority of spread betting companies also put a limit on where you can place an order. Many "ladder" order entry tools allow the placement of a limit order within the spread, but many spread betting companies only allow you to place an order several points outside of the spread.

The same is true for stop-loss placement. Many of the companies place a restriction on the minimum distance away from the price that you can place your stop.

These limitations often prevent the trader placing the order that meets their strategy.

Exits not being honoured

Once an order has been filled it is common practice to manage that order through the placement of a stop-loss and sometimes a profit target. These two exits are entered into the spread betting company's database so that should the instrument price meet or exceed either of these, the open position will be closed. You will often see the phrase that stop-losses are not guaranteed, and this is to be expected when markets gap on opening. Guaranteed stops can sometimes be set depending on the company, but doing so widens the spread. During an intra-day period when no gaps can occur, you will often find that your stop-loss or profit target is met, and yet your position is not closed until sometime later, or sometimes not at all. As before, sometimes this works in your favour, but often it seems that it does not. As we will see later during the strategy creation we will try to factor in this slippage when performing detailed analysis of our strategies.

Position size restrictions

Whilst spread betting offers great flexibility in position sizing, many spread betting companies have minimum and maximum position sizes. Fortunately, several companies provide an introductory period whereby the novice trader can place trades with very small position sizes. However, it is also worth remembering that once you have established your strategy it is only worth playing for meaningful stakes. Conversely, many of the companies also have a maximum position size. For position sizes based on a percentage of your capital, if you find your strategy is hugely successful, or you have amassed a large pot of trading capital in your account, you may find these restrictions come into play.

Overnight interest and dividend adjustments

The majority of spread betting companies charge a fee for rolling daily bets that are held overnight. These charges are also levied for non-working days such as weekends or bank holidays. If you have a short position, an interest return may be paid to you. The interest rates are typically based on the country that the share or index is based in, plus or minus a percentage figure specified by the company. For currencies, the interest rate of one of the currencies from the currency pair is chosen. The specific details vary between companies, so if your strategy typically holds positions for a long period of time you are advised to understand the financing implications of this.

The same is true for dividend adjustments. The morning after a share goes ex-dividend the price of the share will drop by the amount of the dividend. The majority of spread betting companies perform dividend adjustments, and credit long positions, but debit short positions, at the close of business on the day before the ex-dividend date.

Trading ceases under market turmoil

During the high market volatility at the start of 2008 a very large number of traders went short on UK banks. As bank's share prices tumbled the spread bet companies prevented new short trades being entered for these shares.

Why Use A Trading System For Spread Betting?

Trading systems can be used for many types of trading, including spread betting. Many of the aspects of system development and testing used for spread betting systems are identical to the methods used for other types of trading. The main differences between institutional trading systems and spread betting trading systems are:

- The spread bettor is almost always an individual trading his or her own account. The account size tends to be limited in size and the trades use leverage. The preservation of this account capital is high on the trader's priority list.

- The use of position automation in spread betting is relatively new. At the time of writing, only a single spread betting company allowed integration of third party applications to perform position management. All other spread betting companies either provide a web browser interface or a custom application for the management of trades.

- When performing analysis of the system commissions should be disregarded and the spread should be taken into account. The same is true for lots/contract sizes.

- The prices quoted are indicative and frequently differ to the price of the underlying asset. No market depth is available.

- The mechanisms and procedures for managing trades should be geared towards the individual that does not have trading as their primary career. For example, spread betting could be a sideline that supplements a day job.

3

Trading Resources

Overheads

Whilst the minimum requirements to take part in spread betting are an account with a spread betting company and a phone line to call them, the practical requirements to perform any form of systems trading are outlined below. I have called these items overheads because they are an additional cost to the trader. Some items are a one off purchase, but others require a monthly subscription fee and need to be factored into any overall profit or loss.

- **Computer workstation.** Whilst it is possible to trade on the move with a laptop, the benefits of having a dedicated trading workstation with several large screens soon become apparent when you require several charts open simultaneously.

- **Internet connection.** Required to access the spread betting website and the latest technical and fundamental data. Broadband is becoming more of a commodity item and hence the monthly subscription costs of this service have decreased dramatically.

- **Data costs.** Typically an up-front purchase of historical data is required for long duration backtesting, and a monthly subscription for real-time data. Many data providers charge by the type of instrument, or the exchange or index required.

- **Trading software.** Usually the trading software comes included with the data feed but other analysis software may be required, such as Microsoft Excel or Math Works MatLab.

- **Education.** Training courses, books, seminars and newspaper/magazine subscriptions.

- **Office space.** Many independent traders will probably trade from a home office, but some may require or prefer the use of an office away from home.

- **Time.** Whilst not necessarily a financial overhead, the amount of time required to develop, test and maintain a trading system may have an impact on other responsibilities.

- **The spread.** Not often perceived as an overhead, but it certainly has financial impact with every trade placed, and is certainly something that should be minimised. For example, if you placed two hundred trades per month at £10 per point with a five point spread, you would have donated £10,000 (200 Trades * £10 per point * 5 point spread = £10,000) by way of the spread to the spread betting company.

Computer Workstation And Internet Connection

To perform the task of systems development a high-end specification computer workstation will be required. I will refrain from detailing an example specification because it would probably be out of date before this book goes to print since the performance of PCs is constantly improving. I would advise the reader to buy a workstation that exceeds the minimum specification required by their chosen trading software, and ensure that the machine is capable of expansion in the future.

Fast and reliable Internet connections are available from a variety of providers to suit the trader's budget. It may also be worth considering some kind of backup connection as home broadband connections rarely come with service level agreements by the provider. In the likely event that you lose your Internet connection whilst you have open trades, you will need a way to manage or close your positions until your broadband connection is restored. Some popular backup connections include:

- Modem dial-up. Whilst painfully slow compared to broadband it is cheap to implement.

- Mobile 3G or GPRS connection. All mobile operators provide a data connection. 3G allow a connection at almost broadband speed over the mobile phone network. Whilst data costs are typically more expensive than home broadband they do vary depending on your phone tariff. A further benefit of 3G is that you could trade from your laptop whilst on the move.

- Internet café or wifi hotspot. A local access point can provide a useful backup. Also nice to get out of the house once in a while.

- Use a spread betting company that allows you to manage your positions over the telephone.

One of the ways to minimise risk in case you lose your Internet connection is to place a stop-loss and profit target when you open the position. Whilst many of the spread betting companies will automatically place a stop-loss for you, the default values used may not fit in with your risk profile.

The minimum recommended specification to run many system development applications is:

- Windows XP or Windows Vista Operating System

- Minimum screen resolution of 1,024 x 768

- Minimum P4 Processor or higher

- 1GB RAM or higher on XP, and 2GB or higher on Vista

Charting Software And Development Languages

Looking through the pages of the latest trader magazines gives a good indication of the more popular charting and data feed packages. Certainly the two that feature most prominently (or have the higher marketing budgets) are eSignal and TradeStation. Both companies offer high quality applications and regularly provide free seminars and training on getting the most out of the application. Both applications are targeted at the independent trader.

eSignal

eSignal (www.esignal.com) is a leading provider of affordable, reliable, real-time financial market information and professional level tools. eSignal provides a full solution of data feeds, charting applications and strategy development tools. eSignal is a subscription based service and offers a wide range of supplemental services to suit the individual traders requirements. eSignal's system development language is called EFS and is based on the JavaScript language.

TradeStation

TradeStation (www.tradestation.com) is also a leading provider of reliable, real-time financial market information. TradeStation provide a suite of subscription based tools, services, news and fundamental data. TradeStation also has a variety of pricing models to suit the individual's budget, including a forex data feed that becomes free after a certain number of (non-spread bet) trades are placed. TradeStations' strategy development platform is based on an in-house scripting interpreter called EasyLanguage.

At times during my trading career I have had subscriptions to both of these commercial packages and have been very satisfied by the services offered. However, in an effort to minimise overheads, and for the remainder of this book, I will be using a system development application called NinjaTrader.

NinjaTrader

NinjaTrader (www.NinjaTrader.com) is a complete end-to-end trading platform serving discretionary and automated traders of futures, equities and forex markets. The NinjaTrader platform is free to use for advanced charting, analytics, system development and trade simulation. Custom charting indicators and trading strategies can be easily created through the use of a strategy creation wizard allowing a simple click and edit process for developing complex strategies. Further development can also be performed using a scripting tool called NinjaScript which is based on the C# programming language. NinjaTrader has a large community and active support forum, and provides the ability to connect to many free data sources, and subscription based data including eSignal and TradeStation. The application is free to use unless a live trading connection to a broker is required. At this point the trader can purchase a subscription service or a lifetime license.

Additional software

During the creation of the strategies in this book further third party applications were used including:

- Microsoft Excel 2007. For performing detailed analysis of my strategy backtesting results, and the production of ad-hoc graphs, some of the data was exported from NinjaTrader into Microsoft Excel.

- Math Works MatLab. MatLab is a high-level technical language and development environment for analysing data and developing algorithms. I occasionally use MatLab when applying a more quantitative approach to system development, and for the production of multi-dimensional graphs.

- DataBull. DataBull is a comprehensive downloader for historical and end of day data for equities, futures and commodities.

- UltraEdit. UltraEdit is a powerful text editor capable of performing text manipulation on very large files. Typically used for formatting the historic data before importing into NinjaTrader.

- Microsoft SQL Server. Also used for the storage and manipulation of historic data.

Real-Time Data Feeds

Much of the charting data available over the Internet can be classified into three different categories:

- Real-time. This real-time data is the actual price of the instrument at that point in time. Technically speaking the price will be lagging slightly due to the delay in getting the price update from the exchange, through the processing at the data provider, and then back to your desktop PC over the Internet.

- Real-time delayed. Real-time delayed data is typically the data that can be viewed on most finance oriented websites. The data tends to be the price of the instrument at about fifteen minutes prior to the current time.

- End of Day. End of day data receives no update during the day, just the Open, High, Low and Close (OHLC) prices after the exchange has closed for the day.

Trading systems can be developed and operated using each of these data feed types.

However, if the trader is developing a system that will perform intra-day trading, then a pure real-time data feed is required.

The majority of spread betting companies offer the facility within their software to view real-time and historic price data. Unfortunately this data cannot be used by the trading system unless it is possible to connect the data feed into the trading application.

In a later section we will learn how to connect our trading application to multiple data providers.

Historical Data

Historical data overview

Many data sources provide data that spans back over a large period, typically in the order of 10,000 bars worth. If you were only trading on end of day data then it would be easy to use data direct from the data source, as 10,000 bars of data spans several decades. However, if your strategy requires a one minute time period then 10,000 bars of data is just over 2.5 years, which may be too short a period for your desired backtesting.

In order to expand this time period it will be necessary to import historic data into your strategy development application.

Historic data sources for import

A search on the Internet will reveal many sources for historical financial data. Be aware that the quality and price varies greatly. Data can be purchased in many ways, with some sites offering a one-off purchase of a certain range of data, and others offering a subscription service whereby you can return to the site at regular intervals to download the latest data.

One feature of NinjaTrader is that the application stores the real-time data it receives as historic data on your workstation. So, if you leave a real-time chart open for a certain instrument, as time progresses the real-time data collected will be stored as historic data. Obviously this will only work for the periods when you have the real-time feed connected.

If you purchase a one-off block of data you will need a mechanism in place to periodically update the data. This could involve returning to the original vendor and purchasing the latest data, or using one of the many free data sources to download only the latest data required. Many of the free data sources have a large time range for end of day data, but a very short time range for intra-day data.

Reliability of the data is also important. By comparing data from two different sources it is quite often possible to find slight differences in the prices quoted. Bad ticks can also have a noticeable effect during backtesting and can often trigger buy/sell signals where there should be none.

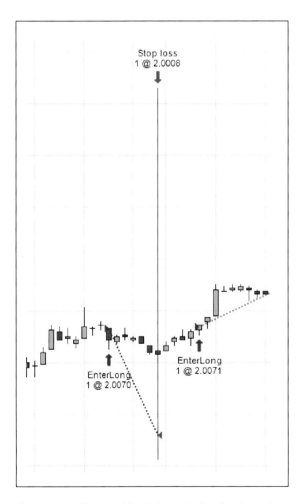

Figure 3.1 Effects of bad data during backtesting

Figure 3.1 shows a long trade being stopped out due to a bad tick before a second long trade is entered. This trade would have suffered a 62-point loss purely because of bad data.

Databull (www.databull.com)

DataBull is a comprehensive downloader for historical and end of day data for equities, futures, forex and commodities. The data downloaded can be output in various formats to suit the majority of charting packages, but not NinjaTrader as standard. An amount of re-formatting is required for use with NinjaTrader. DataBull is an easy to use application and offers a free trial allowing the user to download the most recent six month's worth of historic data.

One problem I found with DataBull is that the forex data does not quote the "Open, High, Low and Close" (OHLC) prices. The OHLC prices are identical for the end of day data. This causes a problem when the data is imported into NinjaTrader as the details for the forex pair are not displayed as a normal candlestick, but instead just a horizontal line is displayed for the day. I did query DataBull about this and they replied to say that as forex is a 24 hour market they do not quote the OHLC prices.

Disk Trading (www.is99.com)

Disk Trading offer historical data for forex, indices and futures contracts, available on CD or for download. The data is available in a wide range of formats, and the Disk Trading team will also format the data to a custom specification if required. Whilst their website is not great to look at, I found their data to be reasonably priced and customer service to be exceptional.

Olsen Financial Technologies (www.olsendata.com)

Olsen offers absolutely everything for the forex trader. They have a wide range of exotic currencies down to tick level over a large time frame. Unfortunately, their prices match the amount of data they provide, and hence are quite expensive!

Data Formatting

Many of the data providers offer data formatted for the major packages such as TradeStation and MetaStock. In addition to the pre-formatted files, ASCII text and ASCII.CSV (comma separated variable) are also supported. These file types can be loaded into any text editor or Microsoft Excel for further formatting or manipulation.

Whilst it is fairly simple for a novice user of Excel to manipulate the formatting of ten year's worth of end of day data, problems arise when trying to use ten year's worth of one minute data. The approximate number of data records for ten year's worth of one minute data is over 3.3 million, but unfortunately Excel can only support a maximum of 65,000 rows.

It is possible to split the data file up into several smaller files of 65,000 rows but this is a tedious approach, especially if you have to repeat the process for many instruments.

If you only have a few data files to manipulate then a shareware text editor called UltraEdit will do the job. However, if you have a lot of data files, the following is an example of how to use Microsoft SQL Server to do all of the hard work for you.

We would like to import ten year's worth of one minute data for GBPUSD into NinjaTrader.

The NinjaTrader import format for one minute (and daily) data is:

yyyyMMdd HHmmss;open price;high price;low price;close price;volume

and an example data record is:

20071204 151000;2.0602;2.0604;2.0602;2.0603;4

The nearest pre-formatted data record that matches the NinjaTrader format is MetaStock:

<TICKER>,<PER>,<DTYYYYMMDD>,<TIME>,<OPEN>,<HIGH>,<LOW>,<CLOSE>

GBPUSD,I,19970522,082100,1.6380,1.6384,1.6374,1.6374

The differences being:

- MetaStock has additional columns for the Ticker and Period.

- MetaStock does not have a column for Volume.

- NinjaTrader has the data and time in a single column.

- The data separator is a comma for MetaStock, whereas NinjaTrader expects a semi-colon.

We will use SQL server to do the following:

- Create a database and table for our data.
- Import the data from the MetaStock files.
- Run a SQL query to output the data in the correct format.
- Save the data output to be imported into NinjaTrader.

First we need to create a database and a table. Use SQL Enterprise Manager to create a database, and then use SQL Query Analyser to execute the following SQL query:

CREATE TABLE gbpusd

(

      Ticker VARCHAR(10),

      Per   VARCHAR(10),

      Dt   VARCHAR(15),

      Tm   VARCHAR(10),

      Op   VARCHAR(10),

      Hi   VARCHAR(10),

      Lo   VARCHAR(10),

      Cl   VARCHAR(10)

)

Secondly we need to import the MetaStock.CSV file containing our data:

BULK INSERT gbpusd

      FROM c:\gbpusd.csv

      WITH

      (

            FIRSTROW = 2,

            FIELDTERMINATOR = ',',

            ROWTERMINATOR = '\n'

)

Note: only use the FIRSTROW = 2 command if the .CSV contains a header, ie, the first row is not price data.

Once the data is imported, the third step is to run an SQL query to retrieve the data from the database in the format we require:

SELECT Dt & ' ' & Tm & ';' & Op & ';' & Hi & ';' & Lo & ';' & Cl & ';1"

FROM gbpusd

Note, we have no volume data, but NinjaTrader requires a volume column, hence we append the value 1 onto the end of our data set.

The output from the SQL query can then be saved as a .CSV file. Be sure to name the file with the name of the instrument. In this example, we name the file $GBPUSD.txt (the $ is important!!)

This file can then be imported into NinjaTrader, as shown in figure 3.2. Should any errors occur during import, the Log tab in NinjaTrader displays the error description.

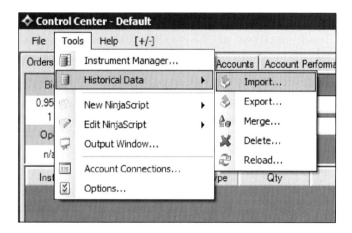

Figure 3.2 Locating the Historical Data Import tool

Independent trader setup

Trading setups are as individual as the trader themselves. Below I have identified three of the most common setups for independent traders.

1. **End of day trader**. Does analysis at home in the evening and places trades the following morning. Does not require a real-time data feed.

2. **Intra-day trader.** Trades at home or work with access to a charting package and can keep an eye on the screen. Trading a market that is open during working hours.

3. **Trading on the move.** Trades 24 hour market, requires fast notification of trades. Has a trading server setup at home that feeds trade notifications via email or text messaging. Has access to a laptop whilst on the move, but just uses it for trade entry and exit, no strategy is run on it. Trading on the move is a little more difficult as it is often hard to stay in touch with what the market is doing. It is important to be able to manage any open position, perhaps by telephone to the spread betting company, 3G data connection, or one of the many mobile phone based trading applications. The trader on the move should also pay close attention to placing stops and perhaps profit targets for the times when it will be impossible to close a trade if the market moves drastically against them.

Trader platform setup

Before diving into trading systems development we should document the hardware and software setup that will form our trading workstation. The configuration detailed below is a common choice to meet systems development requirements and trading style.

IT Hardware

CPU: Intel Xeon 2.33Ghz processor	
RAM: 4GB	
Hard Drive: 500 GB SATA	
Display: Dual Head 256MB DVI NVIDIA	
Sound Card: 16bit or better	
Sound Output Device: Speakers or Headphones	
Internet Connection: 2MB ADSL	
Operating System: Microsoft windows XP	
Browser: Microsoft Internet Explorer 7	
Monitor: Dual DVI 24 inch Widescreen LCD	

Table 3.1 Trader workstation hardware specification

For backup use, the common hardware to use is a regular business laptop with 3G data card. For automated trading a server of similar specification to the workstation, but without the monitors, is required.

Software

I will be using the free version of NinjaTrader 6.5 for strategy development, but for the auto trading chapter a licensed version of NinjaTrader is required.

Data Feed

Within NinjaTrader I will use the free Gain Capital forex real-time feed, and the Yahoo end of day feed. My historic forex data for backtesting was purchased from Disk Trading.

> The Gain Capital historical data provided in NinjaTrader is minute data only, not daily data. In order to get short-term daily data, try using a minute chart of 1,440 minute bars for analysis. However it is not advisable to try and execute or backtest daily strategies against this chart. It is possible to configure NinjaTrader to have a second simultaneous data feed, in theory you could have the first connection to Gain for minute bars, and the second to Yahoo for daily bars. Unfortunately this combination does not appear to work when trying to produce daily charts, and you must disconnect Gain first.

The historic forex data actually comes from the NinjaTrader servers, not direct from Gain. This causes a problem with historical daily data, as it is possible to have a gap forming from the end of your historic data import to the current date. The only way to fill this gap is to download and import more historic data.

Spread betting company selection

I am not going to recommend any spread betting companies as the reader probably already uses at least one or more for their trading. I will however recommend that you shop around. When choosing a company to deal with I look for the following:

- Tight spreads on the instruments that I trade.

- How user friendly their website/trading interface is.

- How easy is it to deposit and withdraw funds from your account?

- How accurate the price data is in relation to the underlying instrument.

- Are they regulated by a financial authority?

- How good is their support both over the telephone and by email?

- What additional tools or information, such as news feeds, or extras such as air miles, do they provide?

Check the popular trader forums for opinions from the trading community.

4

How To Select Trading Instruments

What Is Available?

The following table lists a very small sample of instruments available from different brokers:

Indices	Commodities	Currencies	Options	Shares
CAC 40	Brent Crude	AUD/USD	FTSE Feb PUT	Anglo American
DAX	Copper	CAD/USD	FTSE Apr CALL	BHP Billiton
FTSE 100	Corn	EUR/USD	S&P Feb PUT	Cable & Wireless
IBEX 35	Gold	GBP/EUR	DOW Jan CALL	easyJet
NASDAQ 100	Platinum	GBP/CHF	DOW Feb PUT	GlaxoSmithKline
S&P 500	Silver	GBP/JPY	DAX Apr CALL	Kazakhmys
Wall Street	Soybean Oil	USD/JPY	DAX Mar PUT	Royal Dutch Shell

Table 4.1 A tiny snapshot of the available instruments

Features To Look For

When choosing the instruments to use in my personal trading I look for the following:

- Do I already have experience in trading this instrument?

- Must have a small spread.

- Must be available with the broker I use.

- Must be available in the real-time data feed I have without incurring too much additional cost.

- Must be highly liquid.

- Must have a degree of volatility.

Minimise The Overheads

Spreads

Spread size varies between every broker so it is always worth doing some research to find the broker with the most favourable spreads for the instruments you trade. Normally the spread is proportional to the underlying price of the instrument and its volatility. I personally only look for instruments with a spread of less than five points.

Figure 4.1 shows a daily chart of Vodafone.

Figure 4.1 A daily Vodafone chart between 4 September 2007 and 3 January 2008

Whilst some brokers list Vodafone with a tick size of 0.1, the broker I use lists Vodafone with a tick size of one, and a spread of one point. We can see from the chart that the approximate range of Vodafone's share price for a two month period is about four points (36 to 40) based on a tick size of one. Personally I would not be prepared to hold a trade for this length of time to gain such a small profit. Therefore, even though the spread is less than my five point requirement the low volatility and high tick size makes Vodafone very difficult to trade with using my personal strategies and the broker I use. However, looking through other brokers that list Vodafone with a tick size of 0.1, I can see that the spread has increased to four points, but using the same chart above shows that we now have a range of 40 points over a two month period. Whilst this is still not a highly volatile instrument, the expanded range does make Vodafone more tradable.

Data feeds

In order to do any type of system trading you will almost certainly need a data feed into your trading software. The required data feed and its associated cost will be determined by the time frame that your trading strategy operates on; a tick-by-tick data feed for a wide range of instruments will cost a lot more in monthly subscription charges than end-of-day data for a popular instrument.

As with all overheads, our goal is to minimise them so that they do not eat into our trading profit, but without the data it would be impossible to run the trading system. It is a Catch-22 situation, so the best you can do is look for free and reliable data, or perhaps adjust the instruments you trade to match the data feeds you can receive for a reasonable price.

When I first started to trade, I would focus on a handful of popular European indices and several UK listed mining stocks. In order to trade them on an intraday basis I took out a monthly subscription to a popular charting package. When I started using NinjaTrader for system development I was quite surprised to find that I could receive real-time forex data and several end of day data sources for free. After testing the usability of the data, and researching the broker with low forex spreads, I cancelled my paid-for data subscription and started to use a free data feed, thus minimising another overhead.

I am not suggesting that this approach will suit everyone, but for traders with a small account size, or non-professional traders, this approach is certainly worth investigating.

Single Instrument Or A Basket?

Diversification in finance involves the distribution of your trading capital into different types of investments, such as currencies, bonds, stocks and cash. Two distinctive camps exist. The first says that you should diversify your portfolio in order to reduce risk and exposure to a single trade going against you. The second camp firmly believes that you should have a tight focus by perhaps trading only one or two instruments.

Nobel prizes have been won by individuals documenting complex approaches on portfolio diversification, and whilst I agree that it is harder to get rich by having a diversified portfolio because sometimes the losers cancel out the winners, I do believe that system trading a basket of instruments is the correct approach.

There is a difference between a diversified portfolio and a basket of instruments. As mentioned, a diversified portfolio would contain instruments of different types, bonds, stocks, etc. Whereas a basket of instruments can contain several stocks all from the same sector, eg, five UK listed mining stocks.

In practice I would recommend selecting multiple instruments over different sectors but, keeping in mind the reduction of overheads, I would choose instruments available in the data feeds I subscribe too. For example, if you were to trade the FTSE 100 and DAX indices, several UK listed stocks and some listed on the NASDAQ, you would typically pay for four different subscriptions from your data provider. You could minimise that overhead by switching your portfolio to be only UK listed stocks from different sectors. My personal preference is to trade a basket of non-correlated currencies. Below demonstrates two scenarios using the same trading strategy. Figure 4.2 shows only a single instrument being traded and the overall result is a loss.

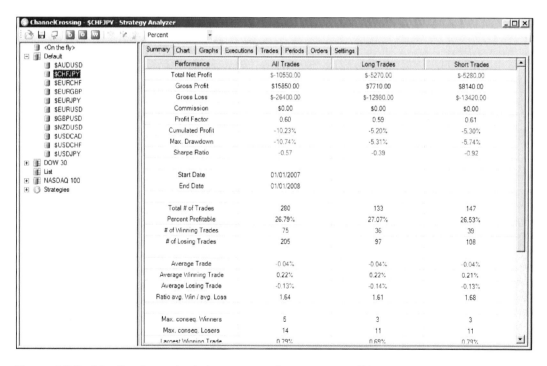

Figure 4.2 Backtesting for a single instrument shows an overall loss

But when this instrument is part of a basket of instruments, and the whole basket is traded over the same time period, the result is an overall profit as shown in figure 4.3.

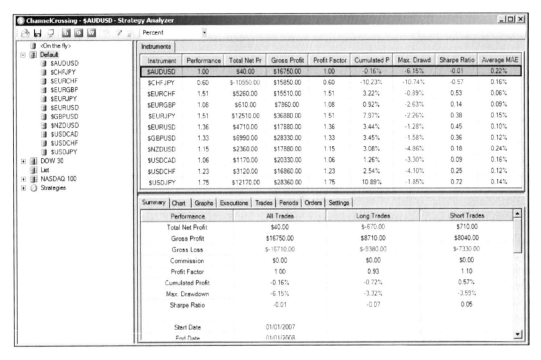

Figure 4.3 Backtesting with a basket instrument shows an overall gain

It is true that the profitable trades have been averaged down by the losing trades, but overall the result is a profit, and it allows us to continue to trade in the future!

Instrument Selection

Based on the information detailed in the previous sections, the process I followed in order to select my system trading instruments is as follows:

1. List all of the instruments for which I could receive free or low-cost real-time data

2. List all of the instruments for which I could easily purchase historic data for backtesting

3. List all of the instruments supported by my choice of brokers with a spread of five or less, or instruments with a spread only slightly higher than five, but with great volatility

Doing these steps creates a large Venn diagram, with the resultant instruments in the middle of the diagram being my final choice for my basket of instruments. For the remainder of this book I will trade the currency pairs detailed in table 4.2.

Currency Pairs	
AUDUSD	GBPUSD
CHFJPY	NZDUSD
EURCHF	USDCAD
EURGBP	USDCHF
EURJPY	USDJPY
EURUSD	

Table 4.2 Showing the 11 currency pairs traded in this book

Correlation

In mathematics, a correlation is a single number that describes the relationship between two variables. For example, if we were interested in discovering if a relationship exists between a person's height and their UK shoe size, we would begin by surveying a number of people and collating the required data. To make the example fair, the data in table 4.3 is based on fifteen adult males.

Adult	Height (cm)	UK Shoe Size
1	180	11
2	166	8
3	175	8
4	173	10
5	183	12
6	166	9
7	176	9
8	177	11
9	180	10
10	175	10
11	182	12
12	170	9
13	175	10
14	169	7
15	177	10

Table 4.3 Fictional data based on adults surveyed

We can quickly summarise the data in table 4.3 by plotting two histograms.

Height Histogram

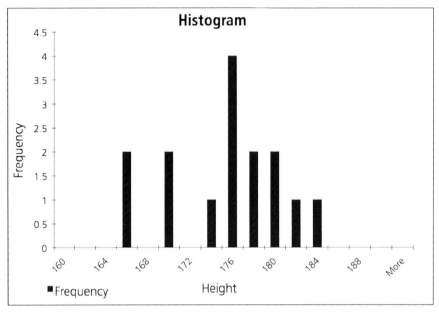

Figure 4.4 A histogram of frequency against height

Shoe Size Histogram

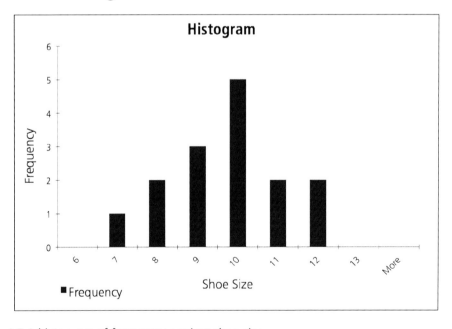

Figure 4.5 A histogram of frequency against shoe size

We can now look at a simple two variable plot, shown in figure 4.6, of our collated data, and it is quite plain to see that the relationship between shoe size and height is a positive one. However, we now need to calculate the correlation value.

Bivariate plot of Height against Shoe Size

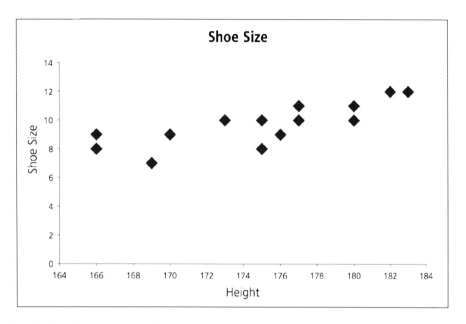

Figure 4.6 A shoe size bivariate plot

A standard formula exists for calculating the correlation value but, as this is not a book on advanced mathematics, we shall use a function in Microsoft Excel to calculate our correlation value. In our data spreadsheet column A contains the 15 values for height, and column B contains the 15 values for shoe size. In an empty cell use the following formula:

=CORREL(A1:A15, B1:B15)

The correlation for our fifteen test cases is 0.798, which is a fairly strong positive correlation.

A value of 1.0 shows a high positive correlation. A value of -1.0 shows a high negative correlation, ie, if instrument A's value is increasing, then we would expect instrument B's value to be decreasing by the same percentage.

At the time of writing an example of two indices that appear to be fairly highly correlated are the DAX and the FTSE 100, perhaps with the FTSE showing slightly greater volatility. The weekly charts in figures 4.7 and 4.8 show their values plotted through 2007 and the first quarter of 2008:

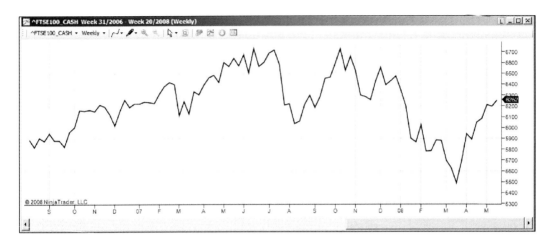

Figure 4.7 FTSE 100 weekly data

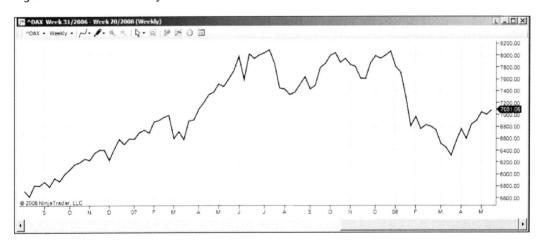

Figure 4.8 DAX weekly data

So how can correlation help us when we are selecting our basket of trading instruments?

Let us assume that we have a basket of ten randomly chosen equities from the FTSE 100. If all ten were not correlated or only loosely correlated, and we traded in the same direction for each one, then some of the trades would be winners and some losers. Hopefully with our trading system's edge and the averaging of our profits and losses, our overall P&L would be in profit. However, if all of our instruments were highly correlated, we could be in the position whereby all of our trades could go against us, and we could suffer great losses. Or conversely, all of our trades could go in our favour, and be hugely successful. Knowing the correlation between instruments can be very useful for the trader who wishes to diversify their portfolio, or double up on positions by using multiple instruments.

Your attitude to risk will determine how diverse a portfolio you will create.

The correlation between two or more instruments changes over time.

Just because certain instruments become highly correlated, it does not mean that we cannot have both in our basket of instruments. It does mean however that we should be aware of the correlation when placing trades. For example, if your trading system generated two buy signals for highly correlated instruments you may be wise to only place half of the normal position size on each trade, or even use the opportunity to use one of the instruments as a hedge and trade it in the opposite direction.

A Forex Correlation Example

The following example demonstrates how to calculate a correlation matrix for five currency pairs.

As previously discussed, the correlation between two instruments will change over time, and it is therefore advisable to frequently check the correlation of the instruments in your portfolio. I personally only check the correlation of my portfolio at the start of each month using this process:

Step 1:

Download the most recent two month's worth of price data for each instrument.

Table 4.4 shows the currency pairs used in this example.

Currency Pair
AUDUSD
NZDUSD
EURCHF
EURGBP
GBPUSD

Table 4.4 Currency pair correlation example

And I will use the DataBull tool to provide the daily currency pair data, as the trial software currently allows you to download the most recent six month's worth of historic data for free. One thing to be aware of with DataBull is that, for the forex data, the open, high, low and close values are all identical. We are only interested in the close values though, rather than using this data to create price charts.

Step 2:

Once the data has been downloaded and imported into Microsoft Excel highlight the Close price column and copy this into a new worksheet. Repeat this step for each instrument, until you have a worksheet that resembles the one shown in figure 4.9.

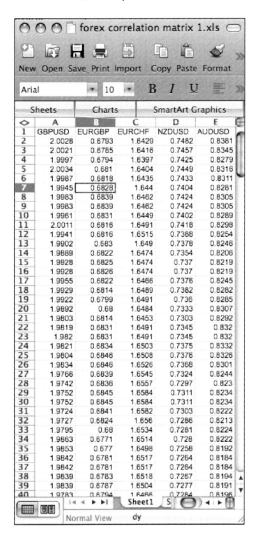

Figure 4.9 Creating a correlation matrix

Step 3:

We now need to create a correlation matrix by calculating the correlation of each instrument against every other instrument. Figure 4.10 shows the comparison of every currency pair against each other.

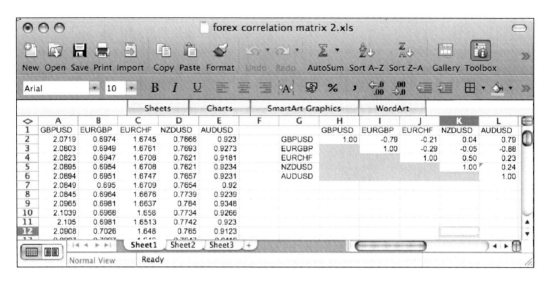

Figure 4.10 The right hand side of the spreadsheet shows the correlation matrix

Our price data for each instrument spans from row 2 to row 58 for columns A to E, therefore to calculate the correlation of GBPUSD against EURGBP, Cell I2 contains the following formula:

=CORREL(A2:A58, B2:B58)

The general formula is used for the remaining cells in our matrix, but the column references are varied depending on the instruments being compared. From the matrix we can summarise these highly correlated instruments:

- GBPUSD/EURGBP has a high negative correlation.

- GBPUSD/AUDUSD has a high positive correlation.

- AUDUSD/EURGBP has a high negative correlation.

Knowing this information will allow us to further evaluate the signals generated by our trading system.

Instrument List

Once you have chosen which instruments you wish to trade, the easiest way to manage these instruments in NinjaTrader is to create an instrument list. An instrument list is a logical collection of instruments. Any instrument can be added to an instrument list, and multiple lists can exist, however I tend to create the list based on the type of strategies I wish to run against the list. For example, all of the currency pairs I trade are grouped together in a single list. Doing this also makes it easier to backtest a group of instruments at the same time. As well as creating instruments with custom names, I also make use of the default instrument list to hold my most popular traded instruments. The default list is quick to access when using NinjaTrader to generate charts or if using the SuperDOM tool for discretionary trading.

In order to create an instrument list, use the following steps:

Step 1:

In NinjaTrader select Tools -> Instrument Manager

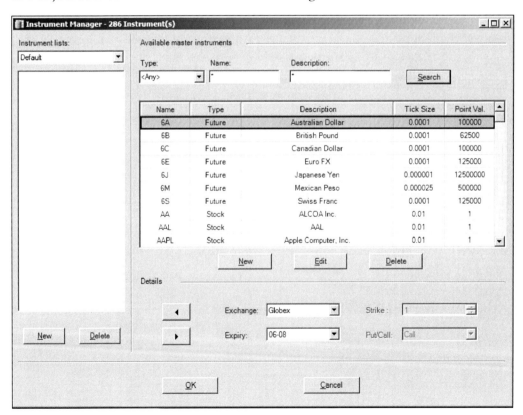

Figure 4.11 The default instruments configured in NinjaTrader of all types

NinjaTrader already has many of the popular stocks, futures and currencies configured.

Step 2:

If the instruments you wish to trade already exist in NinjaTrader, highlight the instrument and select the left arrow to add the instrument to an instrument list. Figure 4.12 shows the first instrument being selected and added to the Default instrument list.

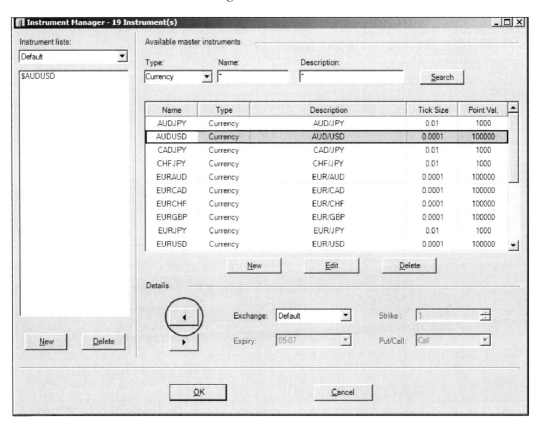

Figure 4.12 The AUDUSD instrument being assigned to the default instrument list

Step 3:

If the instruments do not already exist, you will need to create them in the Instrument Manager. Detailed instructions can be found in the NinjaTrader manual. When creating a new instrument be sure to set the tick size correctly (based on the tick size used by your broker) as the tick size can vary between different brokers.

For example, some brokers list the UK price of Vodafone in pence, ie, 160p. But because the Vodafone share price moves quite slowly some brokers allow the tick size to be 0.1p, ie, 160.3p, and hence the tick size in the Instrument List would need to be set to 0.1. The reason we do this is to ensure that during our backtest the number of points won or lost can be accurately measured. The above example is also true of the currency pairs. GBPUSD has a tick size of 0.0001 whereas CADJPY has a tick size of 0.01. Figure 4.13 shows my complete currencies list allocated against the default Instrument List.

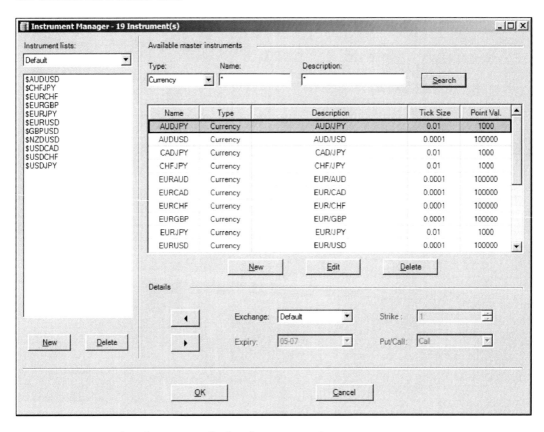

Figure 4.13 A complete instrument list has been created

5

Money And Account Management

This chapter will focus on some of the popular methods for determining the position size for each trade, and approaches for sizing your trading capital.

Progressive Betting

Before we delve into position sizing, I would like to touch on a money management strategy often used by amateur blackjack players called progressive betting. With progressive betting you size your next trade according to the outcome of the previous trade. Different styles of progressing systems exist which can be classified as either positive or negative progressions. For example, in a positive progressive system you increase your position size after a winning trade, and reduce your position size after a losing trade. Much analysis has been performed with progressive betting using fixed odds betting and card games such as blackjack, but to my knowledge little – if any has been published about using this system for spread betting. The general consensus is that you are more likely to break-even or lose a little using progressive betting.

One of the best-known progressive systems is the Martingale system which involves doubling your bet after each loss until you finally win, and then dropping your position size back down to the original size. For example, your first trade would be £10 per point. If this trade loses, your next trade will be at £20 per point, and so on. In theory, assuming you have a fixed stop-loss and a pre-defined profit target, then the first winning trade will cover all of the losses. You may even consider this strategy to be foolproof and logical as you believe that you will have to win sooner or later.

Unfortunately this strategy does not take the following into account:

1. You may quickly reach your maximum position size allowed by the broker

2. You may quickly run out of capital to meet the margin requirement for the next trade

3. There are no guarantees that you will have a winning trade

4. Even if you have a winning trade, it may not reach your profit target, and not payback the amount needed to cover all losses

However, if you do have a winning trade, at a high position size, and you let it run beyond your profit target, it is entirely possible that you could vastly increase your capital. But this approach is very high risk.

I was hoping to show a graph of how bad the idea of the Martingale system is for spread betting, however, even if the trader starts at £2 per point, and doubles every time a losing trade happens, it is very quick to require a stake of £1,000 per point. This happens in ten successive losing trades. Having ten successive losing trades in a trading system can be fairly common especially if the strategy has a tight stop and keeps its trades low risk. In addition to this, trading at £1,000 per point requires large account capital.

Progressive betting, like adding to a losing position, is something that we will not cover in this book.

Position Sizing

With spread betting, the whole notion of placing a trade revolves around which direction you believe the traded instrument will head off in, and how much money per point you wish to speculate. The majority of traders, books and seminar speakers that I have researched, state that a trading strategy is only successful when coupled with a robust money management strategy. I agree totally. By backtesting any trading strategy, it is clear to see that any strategy will go through losing periods. Whilst we hope that these losing streaks will be short lived, it should be expected that a run of consecutive losing trades will occur. Without an effective money management strategy, it is possible to reduce your trading capital down to zero very quickly. Having a poor trading strategy will only make this happen quicker.

Whilst commission is not charged for spread betting, we could equate £10 per point for an instrument with a 3 point spread, to be equal to an average £30 round turn commission cost for a broker, eg, TD Waterhouse.

Fixed position sizing

The simplest way to spread bet, and possibly the most popular position sizing strategy I have seen people use, is to always use the same trade size. For example, every trade would always be placed at a price of £10 per point. I initially started trading using this money management strategy, I know many traders who still do, and used in conjunction with a fixed point stop-loss, it is a simple method of limiting the losing side of your trade to the same value each and every trade.

For example, if you have a starting capital of £5,000, and every trade was opened with a position size of £10 per point, and a stop-loss at 20 points. Ignoring the spread, and assuming that every trade was a loser, then in theory we could be in the game for a maximum of 25 trades (£5000 / (£10 x 20)) before reducing our capital to zero.

The obvious points to note about this strategy are:

1. We should really include the spread in our calculations, an average 5 point spread increases each losing trade by 25%.

2. When your account size gets too low to meet the margin requirements, you will not be able to place a trade.

3. We have assumed that all of our trades are losers. Whilst this is unlikely, it is strongly recommended to look carefully at the results analysis produced during backtesting to see an expected value for sequential losing trades. It is common for trend following strategies to have long streaks of losing trades punctuated with a single winning trade that covers all previous losses.

Sizing per point as a percentage of trading capital

Another popular position sizing strategy is to only risk a certain percentage of your trading capital per trade. Popular percentage values to use per trade are 1%, 2% and sometimes 5%.

For example, if you have an account size of £10,000, and you wish to risk no more than 1% per trade, and you used a fixed stop strategy of 20 points:

(10,000 * 0.01) / 20 = £5 per point

An advantage of this strategy is that as your account size changes, your position size changes too.

If, due to a series of losing trades, your account size had reduced to £8000, your position size per trade would reduce down to £4 per point, assuming that you kept your fixed stop-loss at 20 points. Conversely, when your account size increases, your position size increases, and you always maintain the same percentage of risk per trade.

The downsides of this strategy include:

You will need to either round up or round down the actual per point value, ie, if your account size is £9,000 then the position size calculates to be £4.50. The majority of brokers only allow position sizes rounded to the nearest pound. Therefore at times you may have to place trades that have slightly more or slightly less than your percentage risk value.

If you suffer a series of losses, and experience a period of drawdown, then the smaller position size hampers the process of getting back to the break-even point. This is because you will need to have more winning trades with the smaller position size.

However, the use of a variable position size allows you to stay in the game much longer. In our first example with the fixed position size we had a theoretical maximum of 25 losing trades before we had to quit. With the variable position size, in theory we have an unlimited number of losing trades, as we keep reducing our position size to meet the same percentage risk per trade. In practice, a maximum does exist because we hit the limit of the smallest position size that the broker will allow us to trade. If we are lucky enough to grow our trading account it is also possible to hit the maximum position size offered by the broker.

In the examples above we used a fixed stop-loss at 20 points. Depending on the trading strategy developed, it is unlikely that you will always use a fixed stop value. Later in this book we will discuss different stop strategies and stop-loss sizing. One of the main disadvantages to having a fixed percentage risk occurs when you have a small account size. If the instruments you regularly trade require your stop to be placed a large distance away from initial entry, for example 60 points away, then using the 1% risk your position size would be:

£5,000 * 0.01 / 60 = 83p which is quite a small size!

If this applies to you, then you can either:

1. Accept that trading with a small position size is not going to generate fast and generous profits, but at least your account will not get burnt so quickly, or;

2. Accept a higher level of risk, say 5%, until your account size grows, but be aware that accepting this may actually prevent your account size growing!!

Figure 5.1 shows the slippage and spread adjusted equity graph of a system traded at an initial stake of £10 per point. The stake, or position size, is calculated to be 0.1% of account capital per point with a maximum average excursion of approximately 14 points. Hence, the approximate risk per trade is 1.4% of account capital.

The X-Axis displays the number of trades, the Y-Axis shows the account equity.

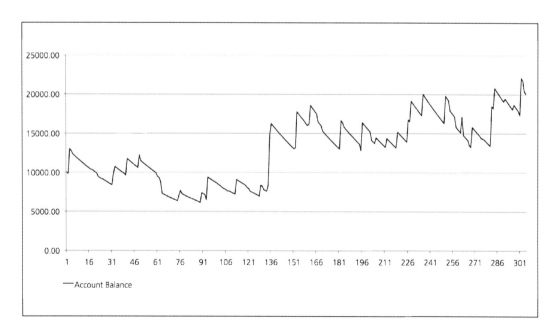

Figure 5.1 An equity curve from a strategy traded at £10 per point

Figure 5.2 shows the slippage and spread adjusted equity graph of a system detailed in this book traded at an initial stake of £20 per point. The stake is calculated to be

0.2% of account capital per point with a maximum average excursion of approximately 14 points. Hence, the approximate risk per trade is 2.8%.

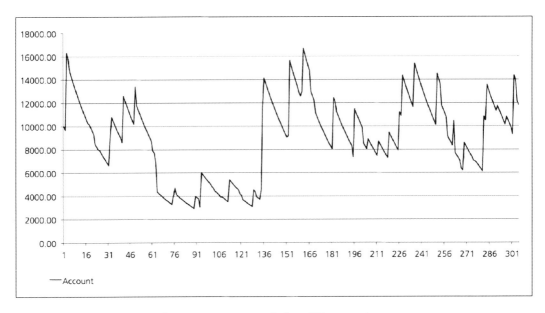

Figure 5.2 An equity curve from a strategy traded at £20 per point

Figure 5.3 shows the slippage and spread adjusted equity graph of a system detailed in this book traded at an initial stake of £100 per point. The stake is calculated to be 1% of account capital per point with a maximum average excursion of approximately 14 points. Hence, the approximate risk per trade is 14%.

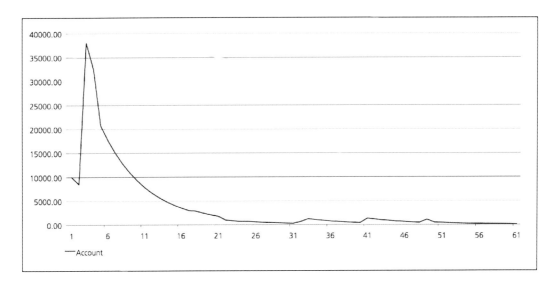

Figure 5.3 An equity curve from a strategy traded at £100 per point

It is clear to see that this graph shows that the trader took on far too much risk, and whilst the first winning trade almost quadrupled the account size, a series of only a few losing trades reduced the account practically to zero after only 60 trades.

Many more position sizing techniques exist. Position sizing is as individual as a trading strategy itself. Building on from the previous example of only risking a fixed percentage of account capital per trade we can also use the volatility of the instrument to calculate a position size. For example the Average True Range (ATR) indicator can be used over a recent time period to calculate the instrument's current volatility. The ATR value can then be multiplied by a constant to widen the range – preventing a quick stop if the instrument moves to the edge of its range – and calculate a potential stop value:

- Stop-loss value (points) = ATR(time period) * Constant

It is then possible to calculate how much you are prepared to risk per trade, assuming in our example that this is 1% of account capital:

- Trade risk (£) = Account Capital (£) * 0.01

Dividing the Trade risk by the stop-loss value gives a position size. It is likely that this position size will be in pounds and pence, ie, £14.52, so it will be necessary to round it up or down to the nearest denominator that the spread betting company accepts.

Obviously these calculations take time to perform. It is possible to automate them within the strategy, but unfortunately not using the basic strategy wizard we will use later. Alternatively a static table could be used that gives a position size value for each instrument based on volatility and account size of the previous trading period (days or weeks). The trader can then update this table on a frequent basis to reflect changes in the instrument and account size. Doing this prevents mistakes being made in the heat of the moment when the trader is opening a position.

Simultaneous open positions

We have discussed potential maximum risks per position, but as we will be system trading multiple instruments with several simultaneous open positions we need to be aware of our total maximum account risk. No matter what system you develop it is highly likely that there will be periods where you do not have an open position for a specific instrument. Therefore, if we have a basket of ten instruments we are system trading with it is likely that, on average, positions will only be open for five of those instruments. To calculate accurate figures for this you will need to examine the "average time in market" statistics found during backtesting. If our maximum risk per position is 1% and our average number of simultaneous open positions is five, then our average maximum account risk is 5%. When assessing this risk it is also worth considering the correlation of the instruments, as highly correlated instruments are likely to generate signals during similar time frames.

Account Sizing

At the start of this book we looked briefly at the reasons why we are trading. Many of us trade to provide a secondary income to supplement life's little expenses, perhaps to cover the mortgage or other monthly bills. Whilst it would be difficult to expect to generate a specific return per annum from trading, it is certainly a good practice to have an idea of potential returns. For example, if you are hoping to cover a £24,000 per annum mortgage from your trading, and during backtesting your strategy returns an average of 20% per annum, it is highly unlikely you will achieve your goal with an account size of less than £120,000. Therefore, calculate the profitability of the system and the hard value in pounds you would like to achieve each year, and then work back to find out the minimum size required.

Fixed size lump sum

The most common approach when opening a spread betting account is to open the account with a cash lump sum and just trade that account from that starting point, adding to the account or drawing from it when needed.

Sizing based on strategy drawdown

Another approach, of much higher risk, is to trade from an account which is sized against your maximum expected drawdown. This involves performing a backtest on your strategy and deriving the drawdown figure from the performance statistics.

Figure 5.4 shows the drawdown for a one year backtest period.

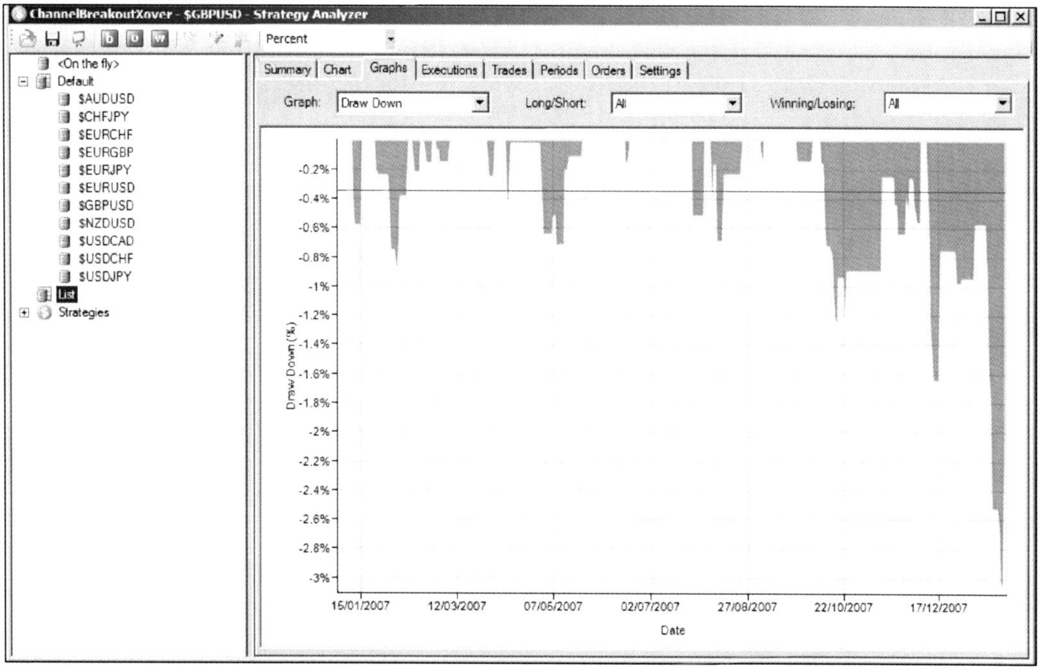

Figure 5.4 Account drawdown for a yearly period

But be careful, the drawdown chart only shows what the drawdown would have been based on the historic data backtested, and your actual drawdown may be much higher, or much lower. It is probably worth multiplying the drawdown figure by a constant to create an estimated maximum drawdown.

For this example we will create our estimated maximum drawdown by multiplying our drawdown by two. This gives us our actual account size required, so in our chart above the drawdown is 3% of our initial capital. Say we were confident that the strategy would not exceed double the backtested drawdown, this value gives us an estimated maximum drawdown of 6%. Assuming our theoretical initial account size is £10,000, then we would only need a physical amount of £600 plus a little extra to cover margin.

Therefore, should we open a position based on our 1% risk per trade, we would use 1% of the theoretical account size. The advantage of this method is that we can trade with a much higher position size. However the serious risk with this strategy is that the drawdown exceeds our calculated theoretical maximum drawdown. Should this happen, then we will have emptied our account! In practical terms, managing your account this way is the equivalent to being almost 100% invested the majority of the time.

I personally would not recommend this account management strategy, however I have documented it here as an option for the trader who is less adverse to risk.

Dynamic account swapping

One of the disadvantages of having a large trading account with a broker is that you are not paid interest on the un-invested capital. One approach to this is to move capital between an instant access savings account and your brokerage account. For example, if you have a trading capital of £10,000, start by having only £3000 in your trading account and £7000 in your savings account. Still place your trades based on 1% of the total value £10,000 (£3000 + £7000), but move your money in and out of the trading account as required. The disadvantage to this method is that it is a bit of a pain shuffling the capital around to meet margin requirements, but the distinct advantage is that at least you will get paid some interest on a portion of your capital.

A further advantage of this method, as many of the traders with Global Trader accounts found out in early 2008, is that sometimes trading companies go into administration, and having some of your funds elsewhere can minimise the financial headache.

Disadvantages of a small starting account size

Starting from a small account size combined with the discipline of money management and a profitable strategy, it is unlikely the quick money returns that many novice traders look for will be produced. For example, if you open your account with £2000, and are fortunate to make a 20% return in the first year, the resulting capital at the end of the year will be £2400. A £400 profit for one year's worth of system trading is unlikely to appeal to many. However, a £400 loss would appeal even less, and becomes a significant figure when taken from a small account.

Overall I prefer to size my account based on an expected return of the strategies, and tend to perform all of my analysis in terms of percentage of capital and the number of spread bet points won or lost.

6

Black Box Systems

What Is A Black Box System?

The non-avionic definition of a black box system is any device whose internal workings are not understood or accessible by its user. In the financial world, a black box trading system is a process that generates trading signals without the trader having access, or a knowledge of, the underlying formulas that create the signals. This typically means that the black box system has been developed and tested by a third party.

Black Box Benefits

One of the major hurdles any trader faces is that of human emotions. Psychology can turn winning trades into losing trades, and can cause a trader to see chart patterns that do not exist. As with any algorithmic trading system, black box or not, trading signals are generated by mathematical formulas, not by human interpretation of price action or indicators.

A benefit of using a black box system is that all of the hard development and backtesting work has already been performed by someone else. Therefore you do not need to have a deep understanding of the formulas or quantitative analysis that drives the strategy. All you need to do is trust the trading signals and the system developer, and manage your trades accordingly.

Disadvantages Of Black Box

Several disadvantages to trading a black box system exist, including:

- You typically have to either purchase the system outright, or pay for a subscription to the system. Some of the systems can be subscribed to for free, but you must place the trades through a specific broker. The broker then passes a percentage of the commission back to the system developer as a royalty. Various other pricing models also exist, including only paying for winning trades.

- Many successful trading systems are designed to target specific types of instruments, market sectors or market conditions. When subscribing to, or purchasing a black box system you must ensure that you trade the market that it has been developed against.

- Often the backtest results published are limited to certain instruments or time frames, and may not be truly representative of the systems performance.

- Many systems traders would find discomfort in not knowing what underlying indicators and price movement generate a trading signal.

- If the system is subscription based, and the trader only receives trade notification via email, text message or instant message, then the trader can be unaware if the formula behind the strategy has changed.

- Some black box systems also allow the system developer/administrator to perform a discretionary selection of which trades are to be actioned on. This may be of benefit at times if the system administrator can see an erroneous signal about to be generated, but it does add a human element back into the system. This leaves the trader with doubts about the system when the administrator is not present.

How To Trade A Black Box

Two popular types of black box systems can be described as either server side or client side.

Server side

A server side black box system is typically subscription based and offered as a hosted service over the Internet. Many, many websites exist that offer a whole range of different black box systems. The majority of the strategies offered are specific to the company offering the service, ie, the website only contains the strategies that they have developed. However some websites exist that offer a wider range of systems from different sources. One of the most popular of these types of websites is Collective2 (www.collective2.com). Collective2 monitors several thousand trading systems covering a whole range of instruments. The service is branded as an independent trading system auditor as they maintain a performance database of all of the systems available on their website so it is very easy to analyse and compare the systems. The systems available have been developed and tested by third parties and then submitted to Collective2's website. Traders then subscribe to their chosen trading systems and the Collective2 website generates trading notifications to the subscriber through email, text message or Collective2's own instant messenger application. Automated trading is also possible as Collective2 is compatible with a large number of brokers.

Some of the strategies have no subscription fees, but are tied to specific brokers. The system developer receives a fee when trades are placed using his system with that broker.

Client side

A client side trading system would run on your own PC. These strategies usually come in a compiled or encrypted format so that they remain "black box" and you cannot see their internals. A client side system would usually be purchased for a one-time fee from the vendor, and you would be free to use the system as you wish, perhaps paying a nominal fee for future updates. An example of a client side system would be an encrypted EFS file that runs in the eSignal charting package.

Are Black Boxes Curve Fit?

It is possible to be very sceptical of black box systems and assume that the developer has created a highly curve fit strategy purely to display highly favourable performance statistics, and hence generate a lot of interest and subscriptions to their strategy. Without knowledge of the strategy details, a set of backtested results over different time frames and a report of current real-time testing, it would be very hard to formulate an opinion on whether the system has been fitted to the data.

In this example I have taken a short period of data for a single instrument. Using a very simple moving average crossover with profit target and *stop-loss* I have used the

NinjaTrader Strategy Analyser to optimise, based on profits for a very wide range of parameter values.

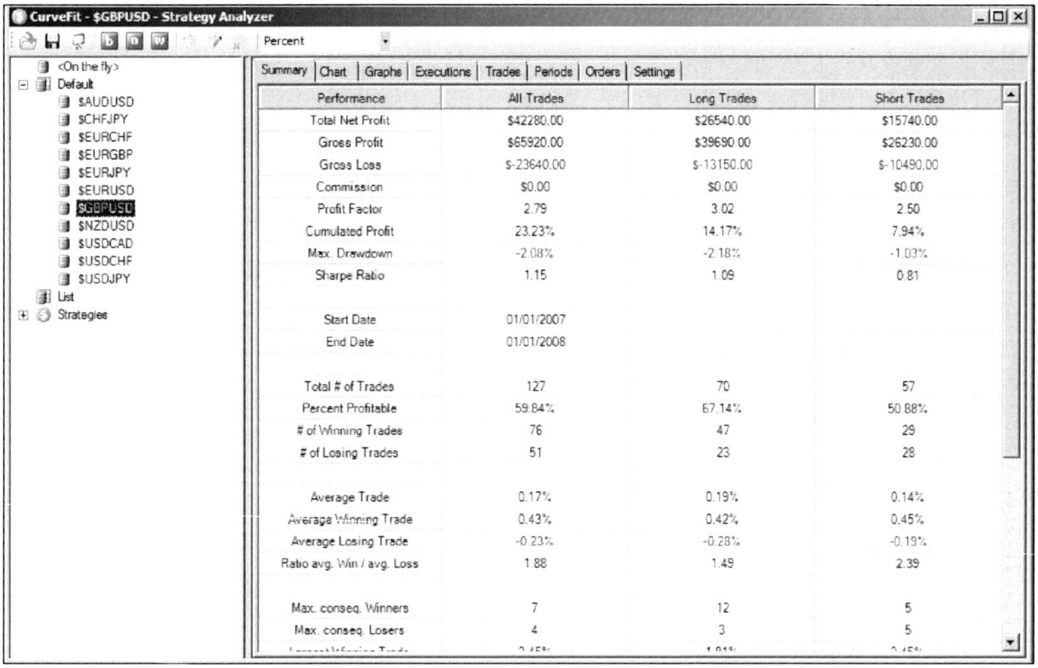

Performance	All Trades	Long Trades	Short Trades
Total Net Profit	$42280.00	$26540.00	$15740.00
Gross Profit	$65920.00	$39690.00	$26230.00
Gross Loss	$-23640.00	$-13150.00	$-10490.00
Commission	$0.00	$0.00	$0.00
Profit Factor	2.79	3.02	2.50
Cumulated Profit	23.23%	14.17%	7.94%
Max. Drawdown	-2.08%	-2.18%	-1.03%
Sharpe Ratio	1.15	1.09	0.81
Start Date	01/01/2007		
End Date	01/01/2008		
Total # of Trades	127	70	57
Percent Profitable	59.84%	67.14%	50.88%
# of Winning Trades	76	47	29
# of Losing Trades	51	23	28
Average Trade	0.17%	0.19%	0.14%
Average Winning Trade	0.43%	0.42%	0.45%
Average Losing Trade	-0.23%	-0.28%	-0.19%
Ratio avg. Win / avg. Loss	1.88	1.49	2.39
Max. conseq. Winners	7	12	5
Max. conseq. Losers	4	3	5

Figure 6.1: Backtest results of one year of GBPUSD with optimised parameters (3,34,170,50)

Instrument	Total Net Profit	Profit Factor	Max. Drawdown	Sharpe Ratio	Percent Profitable	Average MAE
GBPUSD	42280	2.79	(2.08%)	1.15	59.84%	0.23%

Table 6.1 Results of backtest with optimised parameters (1/1/2007-1/1/2008)

Instrument	Total Net Profit	Profit Factor	Max. Drawdown	Sharpe Ratio	Percent Profitable	Average MAE
GBPUSD	15,000	1.37	(3.67%)	0.31	46.10%	0.28%

Table 6.2 Results of backtest with optimised parameters (1/1/2006-1/1/2007)

Table 6.2 shows the results of the backtest using the same parameters but for a different yearly period (1/1/2006-1/1/2007). We can instantly see that whilst the parameters have appeared profitable, the performance results are very different.

Performing the same yearly period backtest, but using a full portfolio of forex pairs, shows a massive difference in metrics between our profitable, and optimised, GBPUSD backtest, and the remaining currency pairs.

Instrument	Total Net Profit	Profit Factor	Max. Drawdown	Sharpe Ratio	Percent Profitable	Average MAE
AUDUSD	13,690	1.58	(3.53%)	0.72	45.83%	0.42%
CHFJPY	(760)	0.98	(11.36%)	(0.04)	47.77%	0.41%
EURCHF	(7,460)	0.73	(6.12%)	(0.69)	42.64%	0.24%
EURGBP	9,660	2.11	(2.13%)	0.8	60.45%	0.24%
EURJPY	(6,090)	0.88	(12.74%)	(0.14)	50.76%	0.46%
EURUSD	(5,520)	0.84	(8.49%)	(0.28)	43.71%	0.30%
GBPUSD	42,280	2.79	(2.08%)	1.15	59.84%	0.23%
NZDUSD	420	1.01	(10.80%)	(0.02)	43.70%	0.91%
USDCAD	(17,320)	0.59	(15.93%)	(0.81)	35.17%	0.47%
USDCHF	6,300	1.24	(4.37%)	0.23	50.68%	0.34%
USDJPY	5,760	1.2	(5.03%)	0.28	48.89%	0.41%

Table 6.3 Results of backtest with optimised parameters

The results show us that the curve fit parameters for GBPUSD performed very poorly for nearly every other currency pair.

The above example illustrates that it is very easy to curve fit a strategy to historic data to give the impression that the system is more profitable than it actually is. Adding more parameters or filters to the strategy would enable the system developer to only select successful trades for the entire backtest period. This would give the system purchaser a totally unrealistic representation of the strategy's performance.

7

Strategy Development – Introduction

Technical Or Fundamental

In the trading arena there exist two distinct camps of trading approach. Technical analysis, based on using indicators to analyse previous and expected price movement and fundamental analysis, the process of researching a company's suitability for investment through the analysis of company reports and news.

The majority of system development platforms rely solely on technical analysis to generate and backtest strategies. TradeStation have recently released an enhanced feature allowing fundamental data, such as EBIT, dividends/share, P/E ratio etc, to be used.

Well Known Indicators

There exists a very wide range of indicators from the simple through to the exotic. Many of these are generally available in all system development packages. This book is neither an introduction to technical analysis, nor is it aimed at the novice trader, so we will not be discussing all of the available indicators available.

Listed below are some of the more popular indicators that are used regularly, and these feature in the strategies presented in this book.

- ADX. Generally used for checking whether the instrument is currently trending or not. Used in conjunction with Directional Movement, it is possible to determine if the price is trending up or down.

- Moving Averages. Various moving average calculations exist. Simple MA's and Exponential MA's are the most popular.

- Stochastic. Often used to determine if the instrument is overbought or oversold. Stochastic does not work well if the price is trending, and also regularly suffers from being unable to predict the point at which the instrument is at the end of its overbought or oversold range.

- MACD. A popular indicator that can also be used as an independent trading strategy. Also useful for analysing divergence and convergence with price action.

- ATR. Used to measure the volatility of the price action.

- Pivot Points. A very popular leading indicator used for highly liquid instruments such as forex or indices.

- Price Movement. Whilst not strictly indicators, price movement and the OHLC values, are used extensively in many strategies.

Understand What You Want From A Strategy

Before you can develop a trading system it is important to understand what you require the system to do. It is very easy to say that all you want is for the system to generate profit, but you also need to include many other important factors, including:

- How often you would like the strategy to offer up trading signals?

- Levels of acceptable risk, and the money management rules you wish to adhere to.

In order to create a successful strategy you need to include all of the lifestyle factors that are important to you.

Choosing The Correct Time Frame

Choose the time frame to suit the style of trading you wish to perform. If you are looking for constant action, then a day trading strategy with short time frames may be best. But if you have a day job then you may be best suited to work with an end of day strategy.

I personally have found that developing strategies that give trading signals once per hour fits my style well. I do this by using hourly charts within NinjaTrader, and having the Calculate on Bar Close flag set to True when I schedule the strategy. Assuming that the strategy I am using is not fully automated, having the signals generated only on the hour allows me time away from my desk during the hourly period.

Obviously, if your strategy executes fully automatically, then it probably does not require constant supervision. We will investigate this area in more depth in a later chapter.

Phases Of Strategy Development

The flowchart in figure 7.1 details a high-level process flow for developing and executing a trading system with NinjaTrader. Each step will be analysed in detail in later chapters.

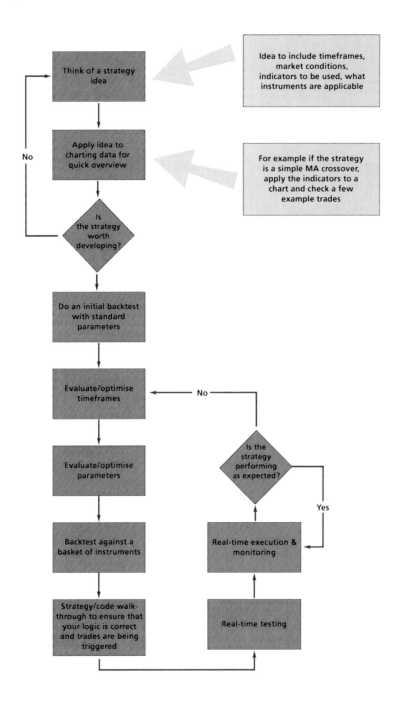

Figure 7.1 Strategy development and testing flowchart

8

Strategy Development – Trade Entry

Establishing A Starting Point

So how do you develop a trading strategy? Perhaps based on previous observation of price movement, or indicators and strategies that you are familiar using in your discretionary trading. One of the hardest things is trying to take your existing discretionary trading logic and turn it into a system strategy. This is especially the case if your current strategies rely on various time frames and drawing tools that are based on human interpretation (such as trend lines or Fibonacci series).

The wrong approach is to randomly take a few indicators and put them together, and then backtest them to see if the results are any good.

The correct approach would be to understand why certain price movements occur, such as trends or breakouts, or to build on some of the popular indicators such as MACD.

If you have a strategy that can be written down as a formula, for example:

- Check that the previous bar close price is greater than the 14 period simple moving average.

- Check that the instrument is trending with ADX > 25.

Then it should be relatively straightforward to take the discretionary strategy and develop it into a trading system. You can do this for your existing strategies and then test them to see how they would have performed over historical data, and perhaps prove their long-term success.

What regularly happens though is that whilst the strategy may have several defined elements that are clear-cut and formula based, there is often some element of human interpretation involved before the trade is placed. I personally have changed many of my discretionary strategies into system strategies and performed extensive backtesting. During analysis I can see that whilst many of the trades backtested by the system are ones that I would have entered on a discretionary basis, there are always a few trades (both winning and losing) that I probably would not have entered had I been trading the system on a discretionary basis.

We will go into detail on trading system analysis later in the book, but I think it is important to detail here the requirements I look for in a good trading system:

- A strategy that has few parameters. By that I mean one that does not require too many input variables.

- A strategy that works well for a wide range of instruments over a long duration, not one that performs amazingly for only a single index or forex pair and only for a short period of time.

- A strategy, including a money management process, that provides a smooth equity curve with small, acceptable drawdowns.

- A strategy that is tradable. The strategy must fit in with the trader's lifestyle. It is pointless having a very successful strategy that provides trading signals on a five minute basis if the trader can only place the trades once per day.

The following sections detail three basic trade entry strategies. Hundreds, perhaps thousands, of different trade entry and exits exist. We will look at only a handful in order to demonstrate how the techniques can be combined to create a full trading system.

Entry Example Using Moving Averages

In the trading packages you are likely to use you will always find a tutorial on creating a simple trading system using two or more moving averages. The basic principle behind the system is to have two moving averages over different time periods. The shorter time period is the fast moving average, and the longer time period represents the slow moving average. The average calculation can be a simple average or a weighted average, such as the exponential average that applies more significance to the most recent chart data, in theory allowing a quicker reaction to price movement.

In figure 8.1 we have two exponential moving averages on a daily chart. When the fast moving average (black line) crosses up through the slow moving average (green line) a buy signal is generated. Conversely, when the fast moving average crosses below the slow moving average a sell signal is generated. Using faster moving averages will produce a quicker, more responsive indicator, while using slower moving averages will produce a slower indicator, less prone to whipsaws.

Figure 8.1 A single trade from open to close

This moving average system is an example of a symmetrical system where only a single position is open at any one time, and the position is reversed when the signals are generated. For example, when the buy signal occurs we open a long position on our instrument. We then hold that position until we receive a sell signal, at which point we reverse the trade so that we now have a short position open for that instrument.

Entry Example Using MACD

Another example of a well-known indicator being used as part of a trading system is the Moving Average Convergence/Divergence or MACD. As per the previous example, MACD is another simple, lagging indicator that uses moving averages to follow trending instruments. The lagging indicators are turned into a momentum oscillator by subtracting the slower moving average from the faster moving average. The resulting value forms a histogram that oscillates above and below a zero line.

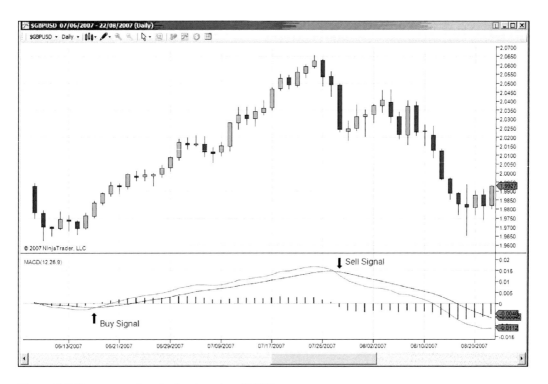

Figure 8.2 One example of a trade using MACD

Using the default MACD values of 12, 26 and 9, of the two moving averages that make up MACD, the 12 day exponential moving average (EMA) is the faster and the 26 day EMA is the slower. Closing prices are used to form the moving averages. Usually, a 9 day EMA (purple line) of MACD is plotted alongside to act as a trigger line.

A bullish signal occurs when MACD (green line) moves above its 9 day EMA or the centreline, and a bearish crossover occurs when MACD moves below its 9 day EMA or the centreline.

The histogram represents the difference between MACD and its 9 day EMA. The histogram is positive when MACD is above its 9 day EMA and negative when MACD is below its 9 day EMA.

Whilst MACD is technically a lagging indicator, the signals it generates are slightly ahead when compared to 12 and 26 period exponential moving averages.

Entry Example Using Inside Days

An inside day can be defined as a day where the trading range (OHLC) of the instrument is confined within the trading range of the previous day's price action. For example, today's high price is lower than yesterday's high price, and likewise, today's low price is higher than yesterday's low price.

Figure 8.3 An example of an inside day

One possible way to enter a trade using an inside day bar is to enter a long order just above the close price of the inside day, with a stop-loss just below the open price of the inside day.

9

Strategy Development – Trade Exits

Once a trade has been entered, the wish of every trader is to be able to exit the position with the maximum profit. A good exit strategy is more important than a good entry strategy. Entries get you into a trade with a probability of success a little higher than random, but a good exit is where you make your money. Several different exit strategies exist ranging from exits based on time or profit targets through to exits based on the results of technical indicators.

End Of Day

A simple trade exit strategy is to close out all trades at the end of the trading day. The times to do this are determined by the closing time of the exchange that you are trading on. For example if you were trading instruments listed on the London Stock Exchange, you would exit your positions just before 4.30pm each day. This strategy is also very easy to test in NinjaTrader as the strategy analyser has a configurable parameter to close out the positions a number of seconds before the exchange closes.

An important point to be aware of when trading forex is that as it is a 24 hour market, the closing time of your charting package may be different to someone else's in a different time zone. The European and US trading sessions are the busiest for currency trading, and the overnight periods, whilst most of Asia is trading, are fairly quiet in comparison. If using an end of day strategy, ensure that you are aware what time your broker ceases trading. With Over-The-Counter instruments, different brokers close at different times.

One advantage of closing your trades at the end of the day is that you can get a good night's sleep without worrying about any open positions. It also prevents you being hit if the instrument gaps against you on opening the following day.

Time Of Day

It is also possible to schedule the strategies to only run during certain times of the day, and exit all open trades just before the strategy stops. So, for example, if you only want the strategy to run between 8am and 8pm, you could schedule the strategy as per figure 9.1. The results are shown in figure 9.2, which confirms that all trades are closed out at 8pm each day.

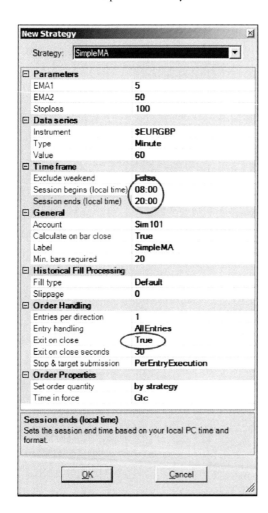

Figure 9.1 A strategy schedule between 8am and 8pm daily

Figure 9.2 Four trades closing at 8pm each day

Of course, having rigid time frames for trading may cause you to miss out of some of the market's bigger moves as you have entered a trade based on a technical indicator, but then closed it because the market closed for the day or your personal close time was reached. During the next trading day, the previously day's trading signals may still be valid – for example the instrument could still be in the same trend – but your strategy may not generate another trading signal so you could miss the remaining trend.

Time of day exits may also be useful if you wish to exit all of your short-term positions on a Friday afternoon before the weekend, or just before major economic announcements.

Before deciding to use such rigid time exits, be sure to have performed thorough backtesting, comparing this type of exit with the other exists detailed here for your strategy.

Stop-loss

A stop-loss is an order placed to close (buy or sell) once the instrument reaches a certain price. The stop-loss limits the trader's loss on the position. An advantage of a stop-loss is that you do not have to monitor your trades constantly.

Configuring a static stop value that you use for all trades placed against a particular instrument is the easiest stop-loss strategy. All instruments have different levels of volatility which change over time. If you were to use static stop values you would find it useful to have a reference table of stop values that you could update on a weekly basis. The disadvantage is that short-term volatility can cause you to be stopped out.

Figure 9.3 shows the first trade being stopped out because the price action reversed. The second trade shows a trade being stopped out due to short-term volatility before the prior trend resumes and the instrument reaches greater highs.

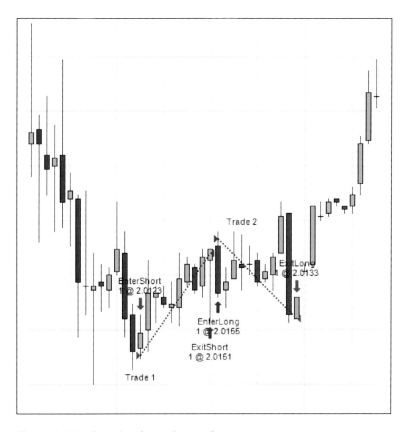

Figure 9.3 Trade exits through stop-loss

Before opening a position it is always good practice to have determined the level at which your stop will be placed, and to ensure that you actually place the stop. Many spread betting companies will force a stop to be created when the position is opened. It is unlikely, though, that their stop value will match your strategy or money management rules.

It is very important that when you backtest your strategy you ensure that your stop sizes are compatible with the minimum stop values allowed by the spread betting company. It may be possible that during your backtesting the results show a promising strategy using a static stop-loss value of ten ticks, but the spread betting company may require you to have your stop-loss a minimum of 25 points away from entry price. As a result of this you may find that you have been forced to place your stops much further away from the entry price, and this may mean that the strategy is no longer as profitable.

Variable sized stop-loss

When discretionary trading, it is usually quite easy to determine where to set stop values. Typically they would be set around areas of strong support or resistance, but these areas are often subjective to the trader. With system trading, an algorithm is required to calculate these stop values.

Low or High of the last X periods

Within our strategy we can calculate the lowest low or the highest high of the last X time periods. We can then set our stop-loss just behind this level.

Figure 9.4 shows the high and lows for the last 14 bar period. These values are calculated using the MIN and MAX.

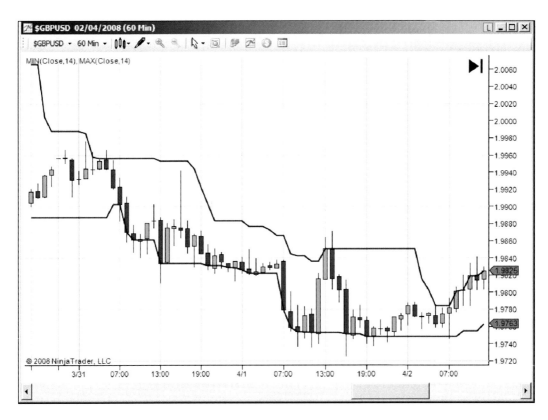

Figure 9.4 A price channel created on MIN and MAX price values

Average True Range

We can use the Average True Range indicator to calculate the range that the instrument has been trading in over the last X periods. We then set our stop just outside of this range, or to allow movement, we set it at ATR * constant.

Figure 9.5 shows the Average True Range being calculated for the previous 14 bar period. ATR gives an idea of average volatility over the defined period.

Figure 9.5 The Average True Range of GPBUSD being calculated

I often use the formula Integer(1/TickSize * ATR * 2) to calculate my stops.

Figure 9.6 shows my custom indicator for calculating the stop-loss value in some of my strategies.

Figure 9.6 Using ATR to calculate stop-loss sizing

The stop-loss calculator shows exactly the same plot as the ATR indicator, but the scale on the right hand side has been changed. Rather than display the number of ticks in the range, it displays a figure that can be used when selecting a stop-loss value.

Moving Average

We can use the X period moving average of the high and low to display a channel. The stop-loss value would be placed either side of the channel depending on the direction of the trade.

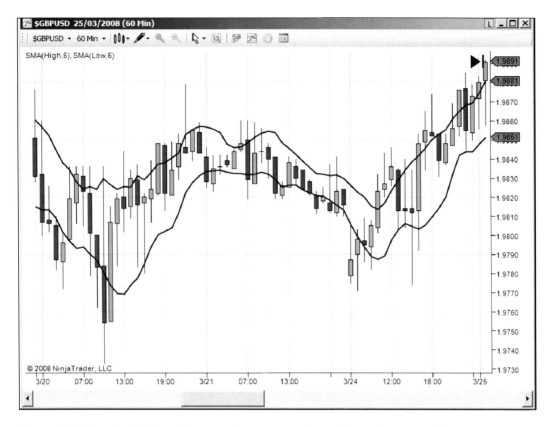

Figure 9.7 Using the high and low moving average to create a price channel

Donchian Band or Envelope

We can use Donchian Bands or Envelopes. The orange plot is the arithmetic mean. The Donchian Band is another type of price channel, with the stop-loss value being placed outside of the channel.

Figure 9.8 Another price channel, but created using Donchian Bands

Pivot Point

For highly liquid instruments pivot points are often used as a leading indicator for price movement. Many strategies look at the pivot points as areas of price reversal. A trader trading the price action shown in figure 9.9 may look for a price reversal at the pivot point, and therefore place their stop-loss just below the pivot point value in case the price reversal does not occur.

Figure 9.9 Using pivot points to predict reversals

Fibonacci

Often when trading with the trend, and looking for a pullback before entering the trade, the trader will look for pullback at the 38-50% level. A possible logical place for a stop-loss is the 78% fib level.

Figure 9.10 Using Fibonacci to predict retracements and calculate stop levels

Trailing stop

A trailing stop is similar in practice to a standard stop-loss with the exception that the trailing stop will follow the instrument's price as the trade progresses. Figure 9.11 shows the position was opened with a trailing stop set to 50 pips. As the value of Sterling increased against the dollar, the stop trailed the price by 50 pips. The price reached 1.9826 before retracing. As the price fell, the stop remained in the same position, ie, it does not trail the falling price, and the trade was closed when the stop value was reached at 1.9776 (1.9826 minus 0.0050).

Figure 9.11 Using a trailing stop to exit a position

Trailing a stop is easy to do in theory or if auto-trading a system, but many spread betting companies do not offer the facility to have trailing stops in place. Therefore, it is actually hard to trail a stop in practice because it requires a manual movement of the stop.

A manual approach to trail a stop could involve the following:

- Set the initial stop, for example let us use a stop that is 30 points below the current price on a long trade.

- Wait until the price action reaches Entry Price + Stop Size, in our case if the entry price was 100p, so wait until the price hits 130p.

- Change the current stop value to be the original entry price.

- As the price increases every five points, trail the stop another five points. Doing this will still maintain a 30 point stop, until the price action goes against our trade.

- Should the price action go against the trade, do not move the stop.

This approach will enable the stop to trail the price, but it does require a substantial amount of manual intervention.

Profit Target

A profit target is a price that the trader feels the open position may reach, and if it does the trader will be happy to close all or some of the trade at this value, thus taking a profit.

Setting a profit target goes against one of the golden rules of trading – cut your losses, and let your profits run – however setting a profit target can be useful for certain types of strategies.

When scalping on a very short time frame, setting tight profit targets and even tighter stops can be profitable as you have clearly defined your risk: reward ratio when entering the trade.

Another trading misconception is that you will never be poor if you bank your profits. Unfortunately it is very easy for the human mind to lose discipline and let emotions take over when a trade goes in your favour. If, for example, you have a tight scalping strategy and your average win is five points, and average loss is three points, and your trend following system is 40% accurate, then how many trades before your trading capital dwindles to zero?

It is also important to point out that if your risk-to-reward ratio is only 1-to-1, and your strategy is less than 50% successful, then over time you will slowly decrease your account size! However it is very possible to have a trading strategy that is only 40% successful but can still be profitable if the system allows the winning trades to run, and cuts the losers at a defined stop level.

Some of the benefits of a profit target include:

- Easy to set, the value can be determined by your risk to reward ratio, or by a technical level on trade entry.

- Allows a clear expectation of trade direction.

The disadvantages include:

- Sometimes a trade will reverse before the target is met, and the position is not closed out.

- The trade could meet the profit target, and the position be closed, only for the price to keep rising. You will miss out on a bumper trade.

Figure 9.12 shows a long trade entry being closed when the price movement hits a 100-point profit target.

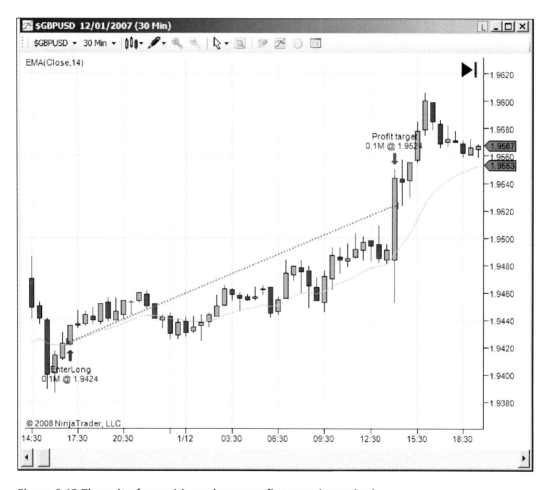

Figure 9.12 The exit of a position when a profit target is reached

Often in highly liquid markets or indices, pivot points (often combined with Fibonacci ratios) prove to be very effective as a forward-looking indicator and are great places for enter and exit positions. At the time of writing the majority of world markets are experiencing increased volatility. Volatile markets widen the pivot point levels, so you should be aware that if you use the pivot point levels for your stop-loss you will be taking on higher levels of risk.

Direction Reversal

Exit example using moving average

Figure 9.13 shows an example of reversing the trade using a moving average crossover. At point 1) a previous short entry is closed and a long position opened. Point 2) shows the long position closing, and the immediate opening of a short position. Using this type of strategy, the system always has a market position.

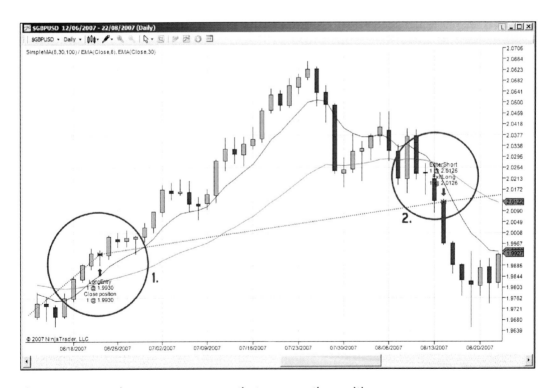

Figure 9.13 A moving average strategy that reverses the position on crossover

Exit using a technical indicator

As well as using stops and profit targets to exit a trade, it is also possible to use a technical indicator to exit a position.

Exit example using MACD

Figure 9.14 shows a trade entry using the MACD line crossing over the zero, or centreline. The position is exited based on a technical indicator, when the MACD line crosses below the ninth period signal line.

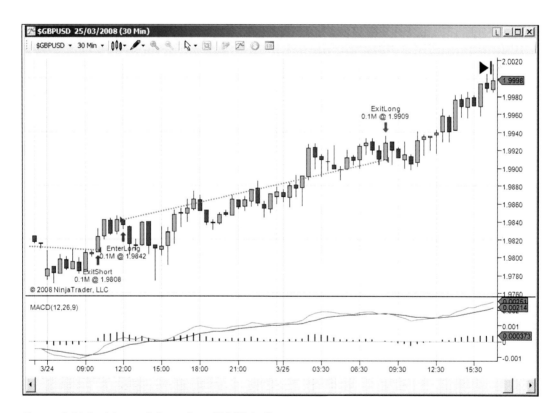

Figure 9.14 Position exit based on MACD indicator

10

Strategy Development – Adding Filters

What Is A Filter?

A filter is a secondary indicator used in conjunction with a trade entry signal to minimise the impact of bad entry signals.

Figure 10.1 shows an extract from a basic moving average crossover strategy. We can see seven consecutive losing trades where an entry signal is given, but the instrument's price eventually goes in the opposite direction.

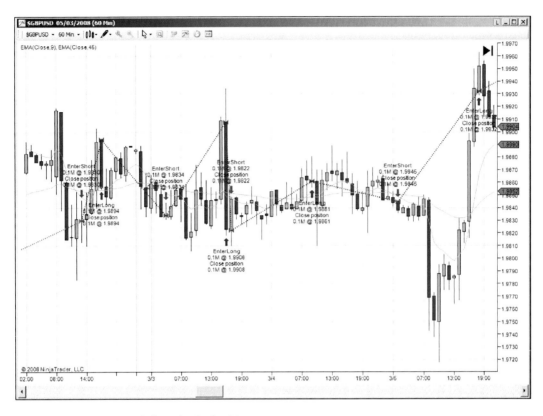

Figure 10.1 A strategy falling foul of whipsaws

These whipsaws can be minimised by using a filter on the entry condition. A technical filter can be created from any indicator or formula based on price action.

As the system in this example is a trend following system we could use a trend detecting indicator (such as ADX) to check that the price action is trending, and thus confirm our primary entry signal.

Figure 10.2 shows the same section of data and trades but with an ADX filter at the bottom of the chart. Often an ADX value greater than 20 is used to confirm whether an instrument is trending. It is possible to see from our chart that during this sideways trending, or ranging period, the value of ADX remains below 20. If we were to change our strategy to combine the two moving averages with the ADX>20 filter, none of the losing trades in figure 10.2 would have been entered into.

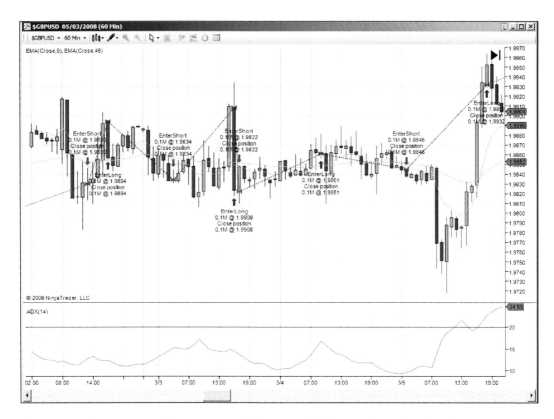

Figure 10.2 The same moving average with an ADX indicator plotted on the chart

It is important to note that the inclusion of an ADX to this strategy may not make the strategy more profitable. Certainly the use of ADX would filter out the seven bad trades given in this example, but it may also filter out some of the good trades.

The benefits of a filter include:

- It provides a screening facility for the primary signals by using additional entry criteria to reduce the number of bad trades, and hence improve the probability that the entry signal will be good.

The disadvantages of a filter can be:

- The filter does not always screen out bad trades. Losing trades will still exist in the system.

- The filter can also prevent profitable trades from being entered.

- Typically using a filter drastically reduces the amount of trade entry signals produced by the trading system

11

Strategy Development – Moving Average Example

This chapter gives a detailed step-by-step guide on creating and backtesting a simple strategy using NinjaTrader.

The strategy is a basic moving average crossover. The theory behind the strategy is to use two moving average indicators of different bar periods. The average value is calculated based on the closing price of the bar.

When the fast period moving average crosses the slow moving average from below, we can expect the instrument's price to be increasing. We take advantage of this price movement or trend by opening a long position.

Conversely, when the fast moving average crosses the slow moving average from above we expect the instrument's price to be decreasing and we open a short position.

Even though we will use exponential moving averages for this strategy, these indicators are lagging indicators, so we should expect to see some movement in the price before we open the trade. Likewise we will also see some price movement against us before the position is closed.

We will not use a stop or profit target, and hence the strategy is symmetrical and always has an open position.

Strategy Formula

Long Entry

Long entry occurs if the EMA(Close[0], Fast Bar Period) crosses above the EMA(Close[0], Slow Bar Period).

Basically we are calculating the exponential moving average of the instrument's closing price for the number of bars defined by the value "fast bar period". If we were to assume that our fast bar period is nine bars worth of price data, then this creates a plot on our price graph based on the closing values of the previous nine bars.

The second half of the formula determines the exponential moving average of the instruments closing price for the number of bars defined by the "slow bar period". For example, let us assume that this value is 45 bars worth of closing prices.

The middle part of the formula, "crosses above", is the comparison argument. The formula determines when the two plots of price action cross.

Short Entry

Short entry occurs if the EMA(Close[0], Fast Bar Period) crosses below the EMA(Close[0], Slow Bar Period).

This second condition is the opposite of the first condition. We are now looking for a cross below the slower moving average.

When we backtest and schedule the strategy, we will use trading conditions to only allow a single order to be open in the market at any one time. Therefore, should we have an open long position, and the strategy triggers a short trade, the long position will be closed and the short position opened. Due to this fact we will not explicitly define any conditions to close any previous trades when a new signal is generated. Should you wish to use multiple open positions in the future it would be good practice to edit the strategy and define explicit close conditions.

Strategy creation steps

Select Tools -> New NinjaScript -> Strategy

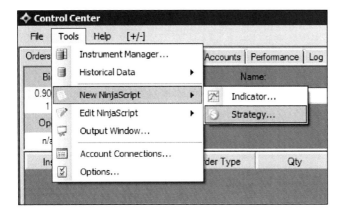

Figure 11.1 Selecting the strategy wizard in NinjaTrader

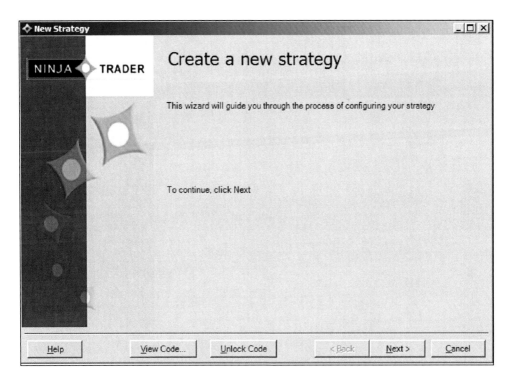

Figure 11.2 The initial screen of the strategy creation wizard. Select Next to continue.

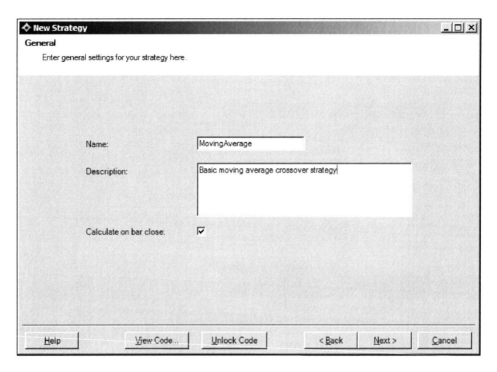

Figure 11.3 The assignment of a strategy name and description

Change the default name and descriptions to those shown in figure 11.3.

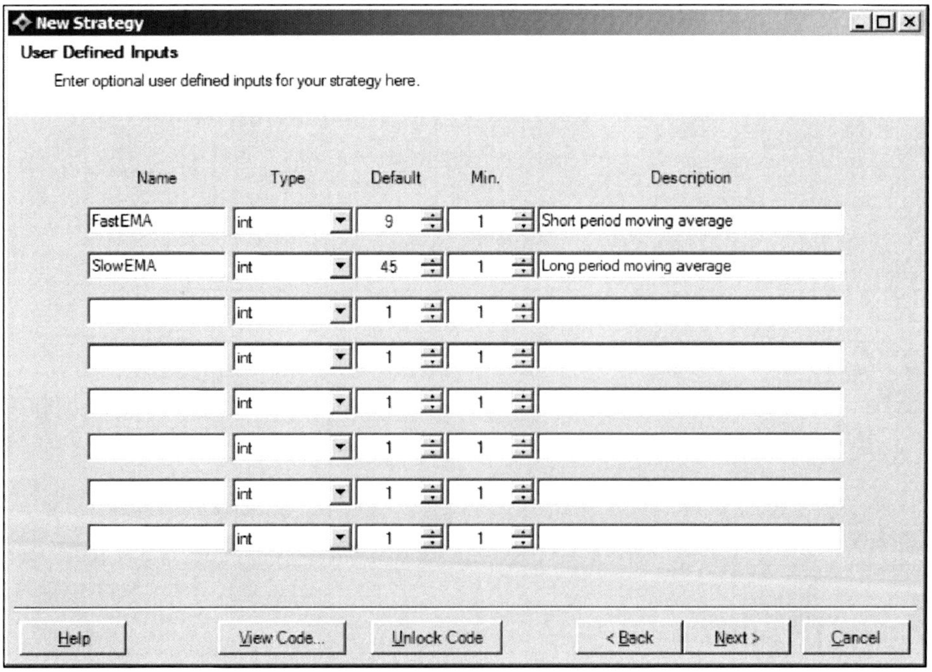

Figure 11.4 The parameter specification page

We define two variables or parameters for our strategy. Each parameter has a default value set. We can change these values during backtesting and strategy scheduling, if we desire, without having to edit the strategy. Select Next when the parameters have been entered.

Parameter	Description
FastEMA	A very short duration moving average value to be used in conjunction with the SlowEMA to exit the position
SlowEMA	Another short duration – although longer than the FastEMA – moving average

Table 11.1 The parameters to be used for the moving average strategy

Once parameters have been entered, the Conditions and Actions window is displayed which allows the entry of up to ten different sets of entry/exit criteria.

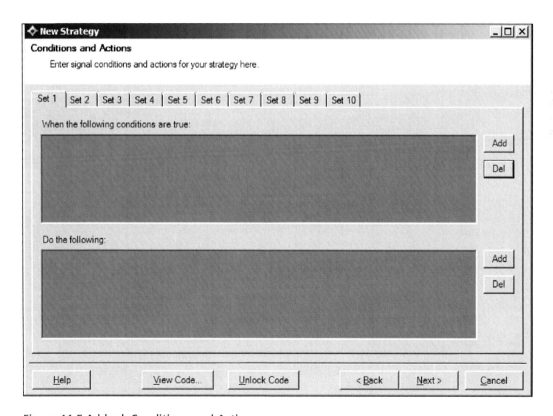

Figure 11.5 A blank Conditions and Actions screen

Each set – accessed by selecting the specific Set tab – has two panes. The upper pane defines the conditions that are required to have happened before the Action – the lower pane – is executed.

For example we will configure the upper pane on Set 1 to be our Long Entry criteria. The resulting action of our long entry criteria is to open a long position.

Multiple conditions can be entered into the Conditions pane. For example a strategy may wish to check that:

- A moving average crossover has occurred.

- The price action has an Average True Range less than a set value.

- The closing price of the previous bar is greater than the current bar's closing price.

Each of these conditions would be entered as individual conditions in the Conditions pane. A logical AND operation is performed on the conditions to ensure that the action is performed only when all conditions are true.

Multiple Actions can also be created. For example, when all of the conditions are true, you may wish to enter a long position, and perform a drawing function on the chart.

For our example strategy we are only concerned with checking our long entry criteria and entering a long position. To do this, first select the Add button next to the Conditions pane (the higher of the two Add buttons).

The Condition Builder window appears as shown in figure 11.6.

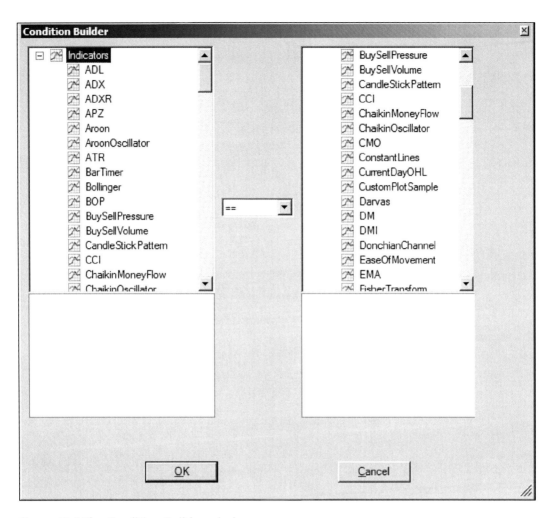

Figure 11.6 The Condition Builder window

The condition builder window is split into two halves, and allows the comparison of indicators, price data, time series, other strategies, parameters, variables and a selection of miscellaneous features.

We are interested in comparing two exponential moving averages. In the left hand window, scroll down under the Indicators heading and select EMA (exponential moving average).

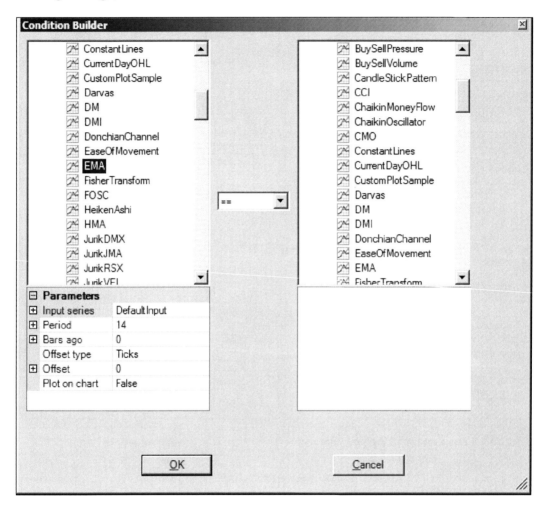

Figure 11.7 The Condition Builder window with an EMA Indicator selected

The strategy wizard displays the default settings for the EMA indicator. We are required to change:

- The Input Series to be the closing price of the current bar.

- The period to be our fast bar period represented by our FastEMA parameter.

- We will also change the Plot on Chart value to be True so that we have an easy view of when the moving average crossovers occur in our strategy.

First, click on the words DefaultInput under the parameters section. A small box with three dots in should appear to the right hand side. Then click on the small box. The Value window will appear.

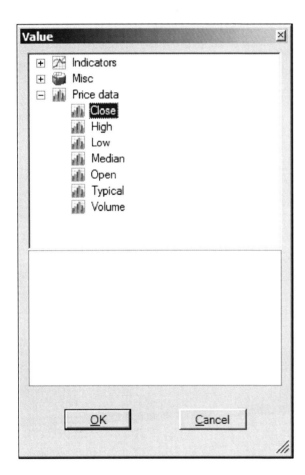

Figure 11.8 The Value window

The Value window displays the different input series that we can use in our strategy. We could even use a different indicator as input, but in our example we only require the current close price, so select Close from under the Price data heading, and then select OK.

Back in the Condition Builder window, click on the number 14, which represents the default Period parameter. Click on the small box with three dots next to the value, and the Value window appears again. Scroll down to the User Defined Inputs heading, and select our FastEMA parameter, and then select OK.

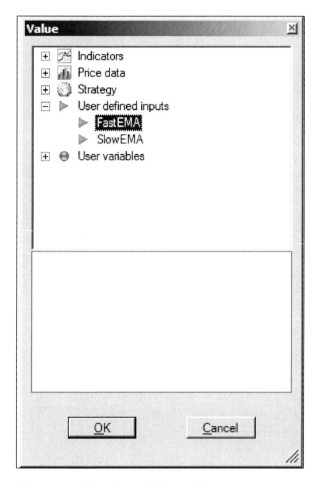

Figure 11.9 The Value window with our FastEMA parameter selected

Finally change the Plot on Chart value to be True.

In the middle of the Condition Builder window is our comparison operator. Change this to be CrossAbove.

In the right hand condition, repeat the above steps, but selecting SlowEMA instead of FastEMA. The final Condition Builder window should look like this:

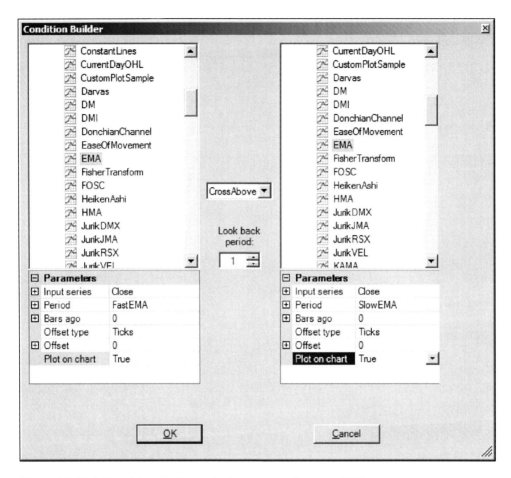

Figure 11.10 A Condition Builder window comparing two EMAs

Once complete, select OK and you are returned to the Conditions and Actions window for the Set 1 tab. The condition that we just created appears in the conditions pane.

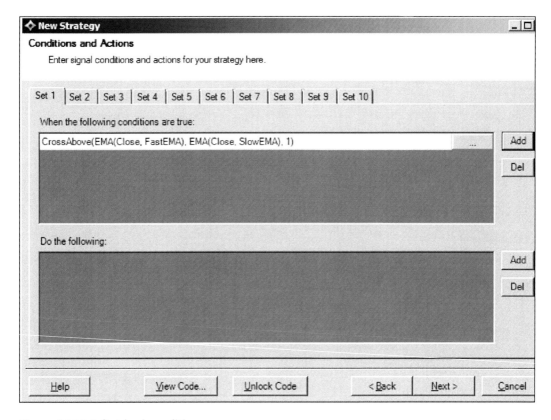

Figure 11.11 A finished condition

The next step is to create an action that occurs when the condition is met. Select the Add button (the lower one of the two) next to the Actions pane.

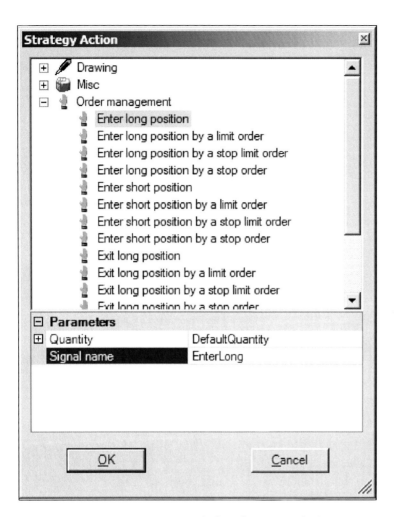

Figure 11.12 A Strategy Action window for entry of a long position

The Strategy action window appears. Scroll down to Order Management and select Enter long position. A parameters section appears in the bottom pane of the window. We are required to enter a signal name for the entry action. I have chosen the name "EnterLong". When selecting Signal names be sure to choose something that defines the action clearly, as the signal names appear in our backtest results. Selecting OK returns us back to the Conditions and Actions window, and we can see our long entry condition, and the resulting long entry action.

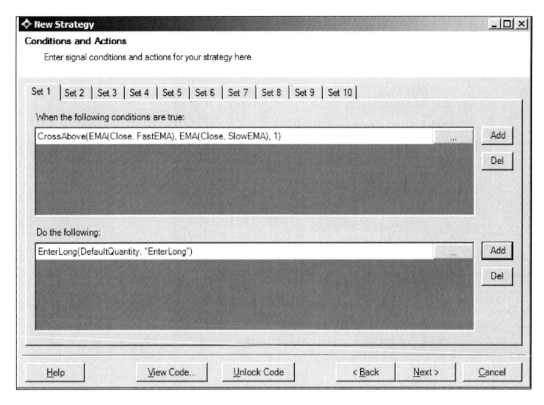

Figure 11.13 A completed condition and resulting action

The next step is to create the short entry conditions and actions. NinjaTrader provides us with a short cut to do this. Right click on the long condition and select Copy.

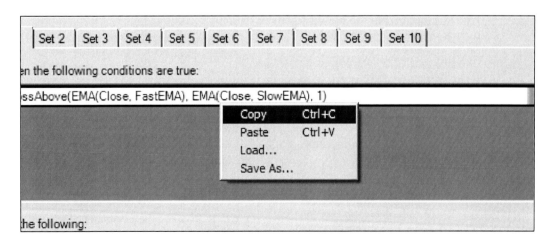

Figure 11.14 Selecting Copy as a Condition Builder short cut

Now select the Set 2 tab, and right click in the condition pane, and select Paste. The condition from the Set 1 tab has now been copied into the Set 2 tab. Edit this condition by selecting the box with three dots next to the condition.

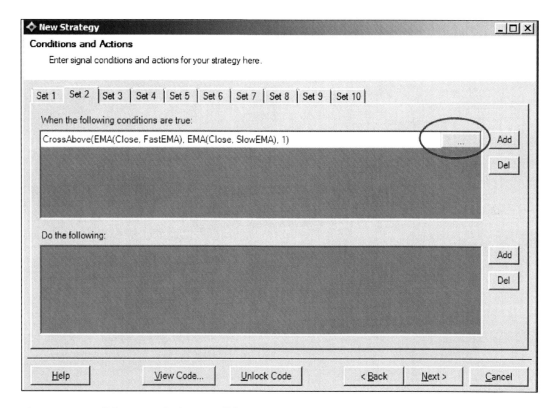

Figure 11.15 Editing an existing condition

The condition builder window appears. For this condition we need to:

- Change the CrossOver operator to be CrossBelow.

- Set the Plot on Chart values to be false, as we are already plotting these values from the condition in Set 1.

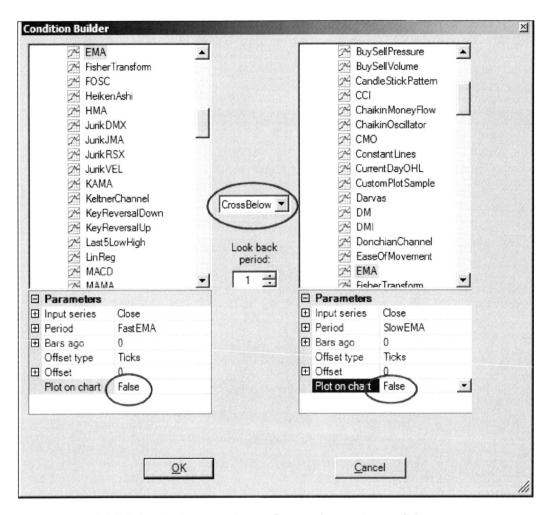

Figure 11.16 Highlighting the items to change for our short entry condition

Once complete, select OK, and we are returned to the Conditions and Actions window. We now need to add an action for our short entry condition. Select the Add button next to the Actions pane.

The Strategy Action window appears. Select Enter short position under the Order management heading, and enter a Signal name. I have chosen "EnterShort".

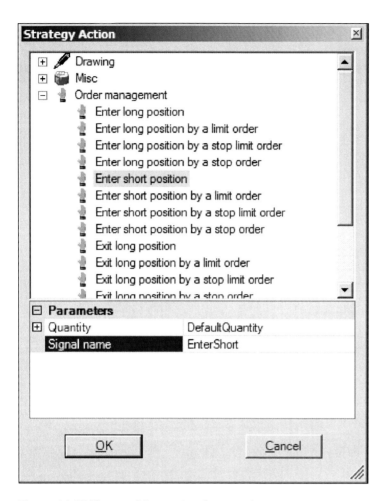

Figure 11.17 The resulting action for our short entry

The completed conditions and action for Set 2 should look like:

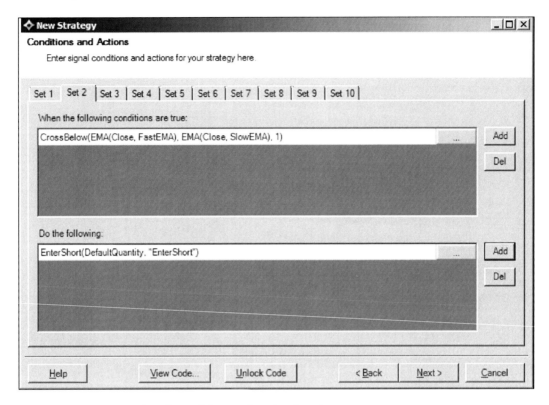

Figure 11.18 The completed Condition and Action for short entry

Selecting Next prompts us with the stops and targets window. Leave these blank and select Next.

The final screen is displayed, and selecting Finish generates the strategy.

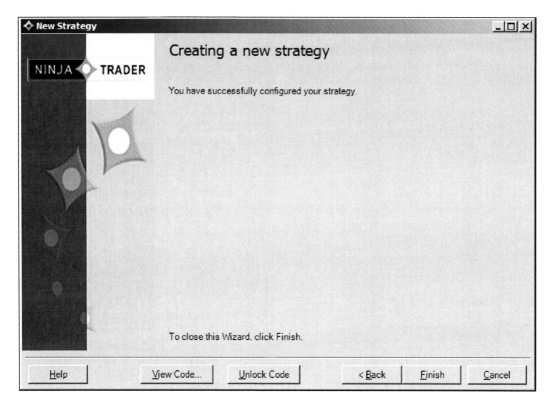

Figure 11.19 The finishing screen shown on strategy completion

Running the strategy

Now that the strategy has been created, we can use the Strategy Analyzer tool to backtest our strategy against the historic data we have available.

In this example we will backtest against the EURJPY currency pair. This section is only a high level view at backtesting the strategy, the next chapter goes into much greater detail about the backtesting process.

I have previously installed eight year's worth of one minute historic data for this instrument, and I have also connected Ninja to the real-time forex data feed provided by Gain. Please refer to the NinjaTrader manual for details on how to complete these steps.

First begin by opening a new Strategy Analyzer window.

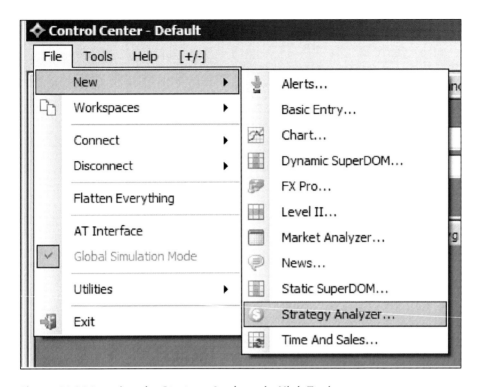

Figure 11.20 Locating the Strategy Analyzer in NinjaTrader

Once opened, the Strategy Analyzer window displays the instrument lists you have configured on the left hand side. In the screenshot my default list consists of the 11 major currency pairs I trade. The majority of the window displays the performance metrics calculated during the backtest.

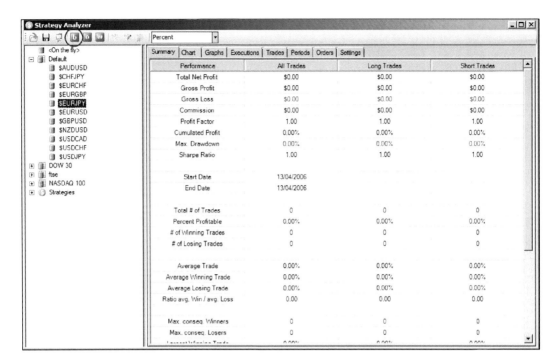

Figure 11.21 Selecting the backtest button within the Strategy Analyzer

First highlight the EURJPY currency pair – or any other instrument that you have configured and that has a range of historic data available – and then select the backtest button, highlighted in the screenshot. The Backtest window appears.

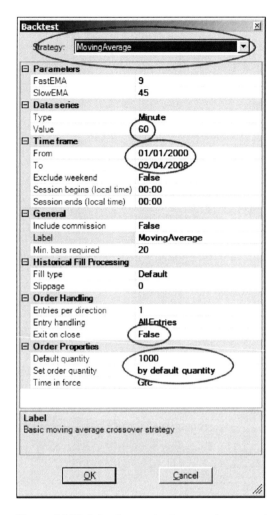

Figure 11.22 Selecting a strategy and parameters before backtesting begins

Before exercising the backtest, I have changed several of the parameters in the backtest window.

Strategy. The Strategy drop down box lists all of the strategies configured in the application. Here we have selected the strategy we just created, MovingAverage.

Parameters. The Parameters section allows us to change the parameters we created. In this example I have left the values set to the default values we used when the strategy was created.

Data series. The Data series allows us to change the bar period on which the strategy is executed. I have configured the strategy to run on a 60 minute bar.

Time frame. The time frame determines what time period we wish to backtest the strategy for. The choice of time frame depends on:

- How much historic data you have installed (or available from your data feed).

- What market conditions you wish to expose your strategy to. In this example we are backtesting against a period of just over 8 years that contains a variety of market conditions.

Order Handling. In this section we determine how many trades per direction, the entry handling and whether the trade should close on exit. I only wish for my trades to exit based on when the moving average crossover occurs, and not the close of the session, so Exit on close has been changed to False.

Order Properties. The Order Properties section enables us to set a position size for the trade. For basic spread betting where we only have a single position open per direction, these values should not be of concern as we will be analysing the results by way of how many points were realised during each trade, and not any overall profit values. However to make the results more meaningful in this example I have set the strategy to choose the order quantity by default quantity, and chosen a value of 1,000 for the default quantity. This is roughly the forex trading equivalent of spread betting at $1 per point for this instrument.

The resulting summary shows a profitable strategy over the time period backtested against. But beware, this backtest did not include any slippage or commission – by way of the spread – or any money management rules. We will cover all of these, and an understanding of the performance metrics, in a later chapter.

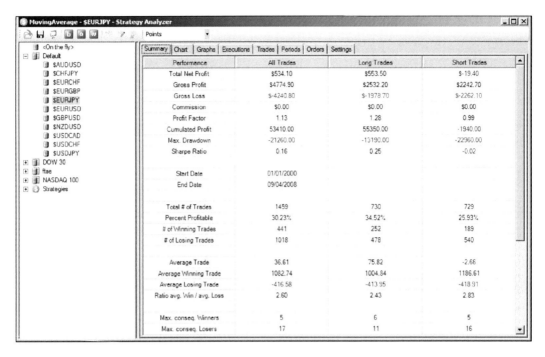

Figure 11.23 Backtested strategy results

Summary

In this chapter we have used NinjaTrader to develop a simple strategy based on two moving averages to create a trend following system.

We then backtested the strategy, for a single currency pair, against our historic data.

Whilst this shows that the strategy generates a profit over the period we have backtested, it does not really show that it is a profitable or tradable strategy.

12

Strategy Backtesting

What Is Backtesting?

Backtesting is the process of checking a trading strategy on previous time periods rather than applying the strategy for the current time period forward. Doing the latter could take many years to perform in order to expose the strategy to various market conditions. Through backtesting, a systems developer can gauge performance of the strategy based on previous market data. This may give an indication of how the strategy will perform when exposed to future market data.

When financial products are advertised in the media you will always be made aware that the growth or performance figures refer to the past and that the past performance is not a reliable indicator of future results. The same is true for backtesting a strategy.

All of the performance data obtained during a backtest is highly dependent on the price movement of the instruments for the specific time period of the backtest. Potential financial risks are raised for the trader who assumes that previous performance results are always achievable in future trading.

For example, a long only strategy backtested over a bull market will probably produce favourable results. Real-time execution of the same strategy in a bear market is likely to produce disappointment, or financial pain.

It is therefore important to have tested a strategy for various time periods in varying degrees of market stability and turmoil. When developing a strategy, it is very important to understand how the strategy is expected to work. Performing backtests will give the system developer a greater understanding of why the strategy did work, or why it did not work, as the case may be.

Having multiple strategies, and understanding how each strategy performs during various market conditions, allows the systems trader to pick and choose which strategies to have deployed at any one time. The trader has an awareness of the current market conditions through analysis of fundamental data such as economic announcements or political events. Based on the fundamental data, the trader can then select a series of strategies to trade on a technical analysis basis. The end result being that the trader has a portfolio of strategies to select from.

It is relatively easy to create a trading strategy that returns a net profit for the time period in which it is backtested. During backtesting it is important to replicate – as closely as possible – all of the parameters or options that will be used during real-time strategy trading. Some of the items that influence the backtested results include:

- The time period chosen for backtesting.
- The instrument or portfolio of instruments selected.
- The price slippage that takes place on trade entry and exit.
- Commissions or spreads.
- Using a realistic initial account size at the start of the backtest.
- Executing the system with the proposed money management strategy in place.

Types Of Backtesting

I regularly employ three styles of backtesting during the strategy development process:

- Static historic data backtest.
- Dynamic data backtest.
- Real-time strategy application and testing.

I work through each of the three processes in order and regularly find parts of the strategy that require modification. At that point I will return to the development phase and make changes to the strategy where necessary, before re-applying the three backtesting phases.

Static historic data

In an earlier chapter we discussed the purchase and installation of static historic data. This approach to backtesting is by far the easiest. Once you have created your strategy, simply use the NinjaTrader Strategy Analyzer tool to run the strategy for a given time frame and instrument. In the previous chapter we performed this style of backtest using the MovingAverage strategy and the EURJPY currency pair.

When backtesting using this method it is important to be aware of the parameter CalculateOnBarClose. I will explain this further with an example.

Let us assume that we have a very basic strategy that opens a long position if the current instrument price is greater than a 14 period moving average. The same strategy closes the position if the price falls below the 14 period moving average.

For any instrument with even moderate volatility it would be easy to see that if we were trading this strategy on a bar period of significant size, for example hourly bars, then it is very likely that many positions could be opened and closed on the same bar as the price fluctuates above and below the 14 period moving average.

This approach may be fine if that is how the system developer intends the strategy to work, however it is likely that opening and closing of multiple positions would just cost the trader a large amount in commission.

Should the trader set CalculateOnBarClose = True in the Strategy Analyzer window, or when creating the strategy, then the strategy conditions will only be evaluated once (when the bar closes and the next bar begins to be formed). Therefore, if the bar period is hourly, then on the hour the condition will be evaluated. If determined to be true (the close price is greater than 14 period moving average in our example), then a position will be opened at the open price of the next bar.

This is a great approach to minimise whipsaws during real-time execution, however it does have a drawback. Positions are also closed on bar close. For example, if you are trading on a 30 minute bar, and 15 minutes into the bar your position is in profit, your strategy will need to wait another 15 minutes before it evaluates whether to close the position for a profit. Obviously, during this time it could be possible for the trade to go against you.

When backtesting against historic data, all of the backtests are executed with CalculateOnBarClose set to True. This is because the Strategy Analyzer cannot "see inside" the bar to find out how the bar was created. For example, if we have a 60 minute bar, the price action during those sixty minutes could be fairly volatile with a large bar being formed, and then close back somewhere near the open price for the bar, creating a candlestick with a small body and large shadows (as shown in figure 12.1).

Figure 12.1 Showing a single candle with high volatility

Strategy Analyzer has no visibility of this price action within the 60 minute period. If you create and backtest a strategy with CalculateOnBarClose set to true, but then execute your strategy in real-time with it set to False you will probably see a noticeable difference in performance – sometimes good, sometimes bad. When the strategy is executing real-time, it has the ability to execute instantly rather than waiting for the sixty minute bar to finalise.

Dynamic data and simulation

One of the problems we encounter with static historic data is the fact that we cannot see inside the data bars. For example if our historic data is one minute bars, when we perform a backtest, our strategy can only perform calculations based on the OHLC of each individual 1 min bar, therefore every trading decision has at least a theoretical one minute delay. This is one of the major reasons why the results of a backtest are different to the results of a real-time test for exactly the same time period.

One way of overcoming this limitation during testing is to use the Market Replay feature of NinjaTrader. Market Replay allows the trader to record in real-time the price changes of an instrument and then replay the data again using different strategies. NinjaTrader provides a synchronous replay of any and all recorded markets and delivers the market data to all NinjaTrader windows as if the data was happening in real-time. It is therefore possible to have multiple charts, strategies and instruments replaying all at the same time. It is possible to trade in simulation mode against this data. It is also possible to vary the speed of replay, so you can simulate several month's worth of replay data in a much shorter time period.

NinjaTrader also offers a Simulated Data Feed which can be connected to in the same manner as a standard data feed. The simulated data feed takes its starting price data from configurable options in the instrument list. The simulated price can then be modified using a trend sliding gauge.

Figure 12.2 The trend gauge

With the trend gauge set to its middle setting the price fluctuates slightly around the starting price. Moving the gauge higher or lower initiates a controllable uptrend or downtrend.

Real-time testing

Real-time testing is the final stage of the testing process before the results analysis is performed. It is important to see the strategy reacting to different market conditions, but because this stage of testing is performed real-time it is unlikely that the strategy will experience many market conditions, unless the real-time testing is performed over a long time period.

I prefer to use the real-time testing phase to understand whether the strategy is actually tradable. The things I look for during this phase are:

- Are the trade signals generated at a time when I am available to place and manage the trades?

- Are the levels of commission and slippage during this phase representative of the ones used during the historic backtest?

During this phase I tend to use one of the dummy or demo accounts available for placing the trades. Not only does this totally eliminate any financial risk, but by using a demo account provided by the same spread betting company I have my real account with I get the extra experience of using their trading interface.

One thing to be aware of when using a demo account is that the prices, price update frequency and the number of available instruments is likely to be a subset of those offered by a full account.

Out Of Sample Data

When backtesting a strategy during the static historic data phase, I tend to split the backtesting into three focus areas:

- Long duration time span.

- Out of sample period.

- Specific market condition time frame.

The typical long duration time span approach is to simply backtest the strategy against a large portion of historic data. For example, since the euro was introduced in 1999 I have approximately eight year's worth of historic data for currency pairs including the euro. My long duration backtest would be performed over seven year's worth of this data, leaving the most current year for out of sample testing.

The long duration data is used extensively during the research and optimisation phases of strategy development. Once I am happy that the strategy is performing as desired, I will perform a further backtest using out of sample data.

Out of sample data is typically a set of historic data not used during any of the development and optimisation phases. Hence the data has not played any part during the strategies development, and can be considered to be clean or new data.

I will backtest the strategy against this out of sample data and compare the results against the long duration time span. A successful strategy will be one that performs consistently over both backtests.

My usual choice for out of sample data is the year prior to the current date, as I feel that the most recent year will be more representative of the year to come. However this is not always the case, even if you have a bear or bull run for a period of years, there will always be a turning point where the long-term trend changes.

In addition to the long duration and out of sample data, it is also worth exposing the strategy to certain time periods that cover specific market conditions.

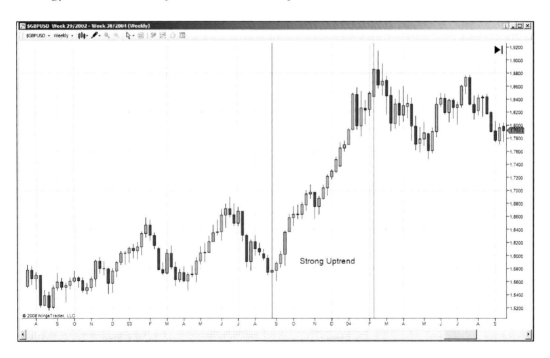

Figure 12.3 Choosing time periods for backtesting: this time period is a strong uptrend

The chart in figure 12.3 shows a six month period for GBPUSD that experiences a strong uptrend. Therefore should you wish to backtest your strategy to see how it performs during a strong uptrend, you could use these date ranges in the Strategy Analyzer tool.

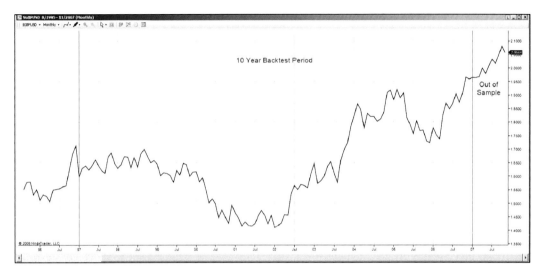

Figure 12.4 A long period of historic data where the most recent year is our out of sample period

The chart in figure 12.4 shows almost 13 year's worth of historic price data for GBPUSD, covering all of the market conditions during the ten year backtest period. Data from the most recent year is used for out of sample testing.

Performance Metrics Available In NinjaTrader

The screenshot shows the results from our previous backtest of the moving average strategy.

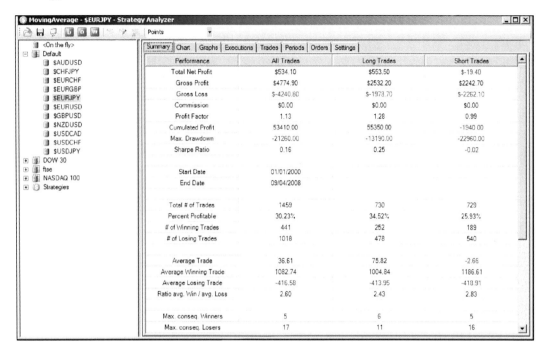

Figure 12.5 Some of the performance metrics available in NinjaTrader

The Strategy Analyzer provides us with important data about our strategy. The different sets of results can be accessed from the tabs within the window.

Strategy Analyzer - summary tab

The summary tab is split into four columns. The 1st column lists the metrics, the 2nd column lists the results for all trades, the 3rd and 4th columns break the trades down into long and short trades respectively.

Metric	Description
Total Net Profit	Gross profit – gross loss
Gross Profit	Total winning trades including commission
Gross Loss	Total losing trades including commission
Commission	Total commission
Profit Factor	Net profit / net losses
Cumulated Profit	Compounded profit over performance reporting period
Maximum Drawdown	The maximum amount of drawdown
Sharpe Ratio	Profit per months – risk free return / standard deviation of monthly profits
Date/Time Range	Start and end times and dates of the performance reporting period
Total number of trades	Total number of trades taken
Percent Profitable	Percentage of total trades that are profitable
Number of winning trades	Total number of winning trades
Number of losing trades	Total number of losing trades
Average trade	Average profit for all trades
Average winning trade	Average profit for all winning trades
Average losing trade	The average loss for all losing trades
Ratio of Avg. Win/Avg. Loss	Win/loss ratio
Max consecutive winners	The maximum number of consecutive winning trades
Max consecutive losers	The maximum number of consecutive losing trades
Largest winning trade	The largest winning trade
Largest losing trade	The largest losing trade
Number of trades per day	Total number of trades divided by total number of days in the performance reporting period
Avg. time in market	The average time in days that each trade is in the market
Avg. bars in trade	Avg. bars in trade
Profit per month	Profit per month
Max. time to recover	The maximum time in days that it takes to recover from a drawdown, ie, to get back to break-even
Average MAE	Average maximum adverse excursion which represents the worst loss level a trade reached
Average MFE	Average maximum favourable excursion which represents the best profit level a trade reached
Average ETD	The average End Trade Drawdown

Table 12.1 Performance Metrics available in NinjaTrader and their respective descriptions

Possible metrics to observe

When creating a trading system for the first time it is easy to focus on the total net profit and the percentage profitable figures.

Total net profit

Total net profit is the sum of all of the losing trades (gross losses) subtracted from the sum of all of the winning trades (gross profits). Sometimes this can be an ego-boosting figure, although I would recommend that it is only used as a guide because the actual figures obtained, when the strategy is run real-time, can be very different. It should also be noted that strategies created using the wizard do not have access to any money management facilities, so you will be unable to position size your trades correctly based on available account capital.

Percentage profitable

Percentage profitable can also be a misleading figure. Whilst it is highly desirable to have a strategy with a high probability of success, using a proper money management approach can allow the trader to have a low percentage of profitable trades and yet still return an overall profit. Typically a trend following strategy will have a high percentage of losing trades which are stopped out or closed for a small loss, and a small percentage of large successful trades.

Better metrics to observe

This section details the performance metrics that I focus on during the results analysis phase of backtesting. A key point to make is that not one single metric should be looked at in isolation as each one has their benefits and drawbacks. It is also rare to find a system that exhibits healthy values for each of the performance metrics. Many systems will have positive results in certain areas, but then experience poor statistics for another metric. Compromise and discretion play a large part in choosing the final strategy to trade with.

Profit factor

The profit factor can be calculated by dividing the gross profits value by the gross losses. For example the total dollars gained on all of the winning trades divided by the total dollars lost on all of the losing trades. For spread betting we can substitute dollars for points, thus removing any discrepancy that may occur in the backtest results due to different position sizes.

A profit factor greater than one indicates that the system returned a profit during the backtest period. A value less than one shows that the system made a loss.

One of the problems with using profit factor is that it does not give an indication of the tradability of the system. For example, you may have a trend following strategy that has an average successful trade of 1 in 5.

Trade	Profit/Loss (points)
Trade 1	-10
Trade 2	-10
Trade 3	60
Trade 4	-10
Trade 5	-10

Table 12.2 Sample trade results

The table shows that we had four losing trades, each losing 10 points. The single winning trade returned a profit of 60 points.

60 (gross profit) / 40 (gross loss) = 1.5 (Profit Factor)

The strategy returns a positive profit factor value, and is reasonably stable by way of it receiving several small value losing trades. Thus cutting our losses and letting our profits run.

In comparison, we could take a second strategy.

Trade	Profit/Loss (points)
Trade 1	100
Trade 2	-100
Trade 3	100
Trade 4	-100
Trade 5	100
Trade 6	-100
Trade 7	100
Trade 8	65

Table 12.3 Sample trade results

The table shows that we had three losing trades, each losing 100 points each. The winning trades returned a profit of 465 points.

465 (gross profit) / 300 (gross loss) = 1.5 (Profit Factor)

The strategy returns a positive profit factor value, but has a massive swing between winning and losing trades. This high volatility may lead to a system being deemed to be "untradeable", yet it has the same profit factor as our first strategy.

Sharpe Ratio

The Sharpe Ratio is a measure of the excess return per unit of risk in a trading system. Developed by William Sharpe, the Sharpe Ratio tells us whether the returns from a portfolio are due to intelligent investment decisions (sensible strategy partnered with good money management), or the result of excess risk (large position sizing out of proportion with available capital). The Sharpe Ratio is a useful metric when comparing the performance of two strategies, especially if one appears to have a much higher return, as the ratio enables us to see if that higher return is because of a higher risk. The higher the Sharpe Ratio metric, the better the risk-adjusted performance of the strategy.

Average maximum adverse excursion

The maximum adverse excursion represents the largest loss (realised or unrealised) suffered by a single trade during the backtest period. For example if an open trade goes against the trader, falls to a 50 point loss, and then recovers for a smaller loss or even a profit, then the MAE for that trade will be 50 points. It is worth noting that NinjaTrader does not display the figure as a negative value. It is assumed that because the figure is the Adverse Excursion, rather than Favourable Excursion, the figure is negative.

The average MAE is the mean value of all of the MAEs, and therefore gives a single averaged figure for the backtest period. As the figure is an average, the system trader must be aware that larger and smaller losses will occur than the average MAE value.

Typically a strategy that has a tight stop-loss will see the average MAE metric to be close to the stop-loss value, as the stop is likely to be hit before a technical indicator closes a losing trade.

A small average MAE is desirable in a strategy.

Strategy Analyzer – chart tab

The Chart tab displays the instruments price data for the backtested period. All positions are detailed on the chart, including any plots from the strategy. Additional indicators and drawing tools can be used on the chart for further analysis.

Figure 12.6 The chart, indicators and trades for a backtested instrument

Strategy Analyzer – graphs tab

The graphs tab details several useful graphs of the trades during the backtest period. The two graphs that I find most useful are the Cumulated Profit and the Drawdown graphs. The Cumulated Profit graph provides details of the equity curve.

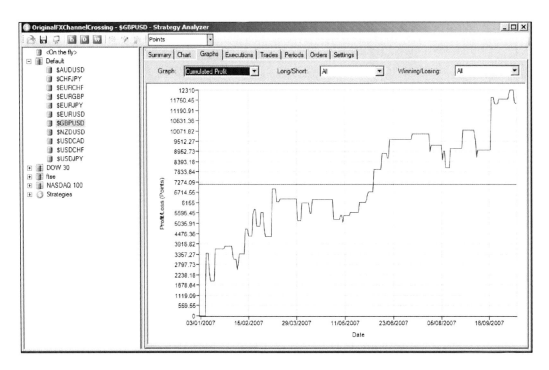

Figure 12.7 A large profit from an early trade, and then a steady – but not smooth – equity curve

Equity curves tend to smooth out when a higher number of trades, or a longer time period is used.

The drawdown plots the drawdown for the backtest period.

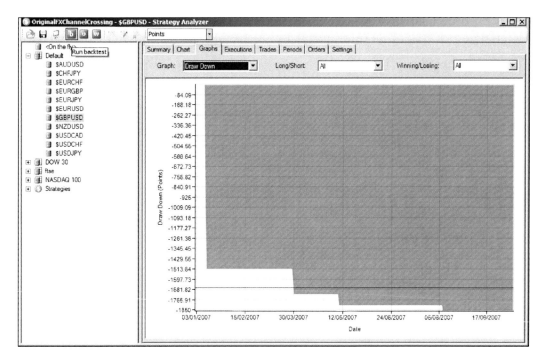

Figure 12.8 A large drawdown early into the backtest

Strategy Analyzer – trades tab

The Trades tab details all of the trades during the backtest period. The data from this tab will be exported into Excel during our detailed backtesting analysis.

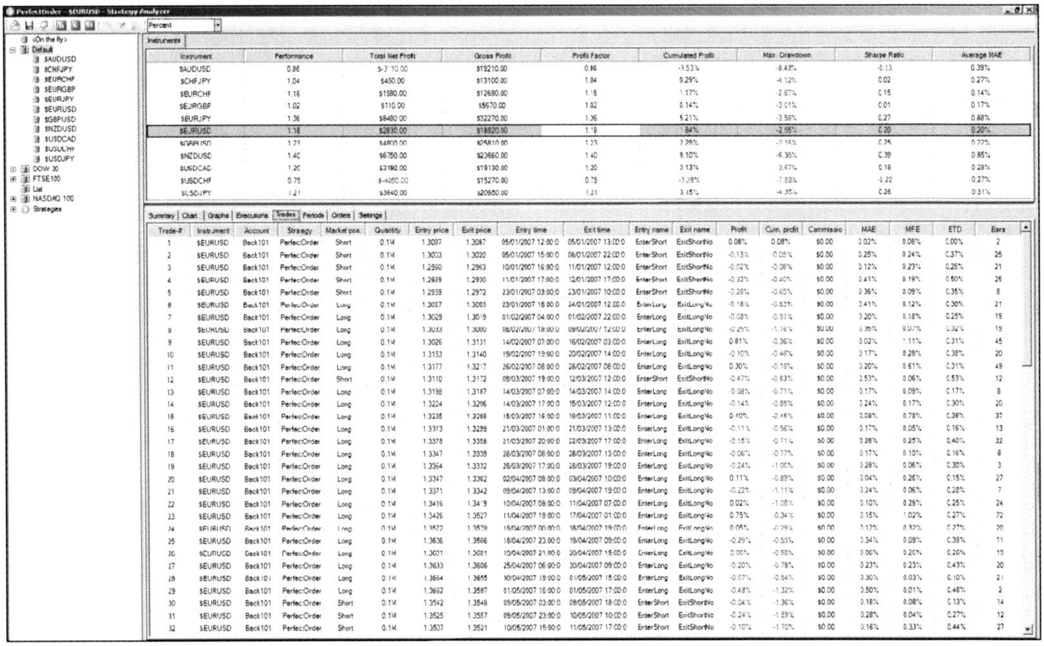

Figure 12.9 An example trades tab displaying all of the trade details for that instrument during the backtest

Slippage

Slippage can be defined as the change in price that occurs between the time when the trading system notifies the trader of a trade, and the time when the position is actually filled. Slippage occurs on both the opening and closing of positions. When systems trading for spread betting, slippage can be further broken down into three areas:

1. The time between the trading system generating a signal, and the trader receiving the signal.

2. The time between the trader receiving the signal and the order being placed with the spread betting company.

3. The time between the trader placing the order, and the order being filled.

The time taken for a trader to receive a trading signal from the system and the placing of the trade depends on the system setup and its tradability. If the trader, trading system and order entry tool are all accessible from the trading workstation, and the trader is watching the markets, then this slippage can be minimal in all but the fastest moving markets.

Should the trader be reliant on an email generated by the trading system, a high degree of latency can be expected, and the position may be entered a matter of minutes or more after the signal was generated. Tradability issues due to trade notification will be uncovered during real-time testing of the strategy.

The final area of slippage, the slippage generated while the order is being filled by the spread betting company, is out of the hands of the trader. Only experience will determine how the trader perceives the speed at which his orders are filled.

With automated trading slippage still exists, but to a lesser extent.

13

Strategy Optimisation

Optimisation Overview

Strategy optimisation is the process of taking a successful strategy and performing further backtests (but each additional backtest varies the input parameters and/or the bar period ie, an hourly bar chart), to understand the optimum parameters for the trading system.

Taking our example Moving Average strategy from a previous chapter, we have the following parameters that we can change:

Parameter	Description
FastEMA	A very short duration moving average value to be used in conjunction with the SlowEMA to exit the position
SlowEMA	Another short duration (although longer than the FastEMA) moving average

Table 13.1 Moving average parameters used in an earlier strategy example

Our previous backtest also used only a 60 minute bar period. During the optimisation of this strategy we should also consider different bar periods.

During our optimisation of the Moving Average strategy, we will vary both of the input parameters using the Optimise feature of the NinjaTrader Strategy Analyzer. We will also backtest several different bar periods. At the time of writing, the current version of NinjaTrader does not support optimisation based on time, hence this step will be a manual process.

Backtesting a strategy is a long process, optimising a strategy takes even longer!

Before starting the optimisation process, it is worth a quick reminder that it is possible to over-optimise a strategy and effectively curve fit the strategy to the data. Remember that we are looking to produce a finalised strategy that uses the same parameters and time period, yet works for a range of instruments.

When optimising a strategy I usually employ two techniques. The first is to use the optimisation feature of NinjaTrader to perform a backtest on every single input parameter I set for the strategy. The second technique is to be more selective on input parameters and bar periods, exercise each backtest based on those parameters, and plot the results as a graph in MS Excel or MatLab.

Whilst I believe that the second approach does produce a slightly better result, it does take an extremely large amount of effort, and would possibly go into a depth of complexity outside the scope of this book. A further benefit of this approach is that having to manually choose the parameters does give the system developer a greater insight into the inner workings of their strategy.

Backtesting And Optimising Example Using Moving Averages

Automated optimisation with NinjaTrader

Taking our two exponential moving average parameters as a starting point we should decide which input ranges to choose. The moving average strategy uses the crossover of two different period moving averages to spot the trends and hence trigger the trades.

The fast moving average is likely to be a short duration, perhaps with a bar period of less than 10. The slow moving average will be a longer duration of a higher range of values. The step value determines how the parameter value will be incremented for each optimised backtest.

For example, if we were to use the input parameter 3;10;1 for FastEMA we are telling the optimiser to use a starting value of 3, an end value of 10, and an increment of 1. Therefore the optimiser would use values 3 through to 10 (ie, all of the values 3,4,5,6,7,8,9 and 10) one at a time.

For our second input parameter, SlowEMA, if we were to use 20;60;5 we are telling the optimiser to start at the value 20 and finish at the value 60, incrementing the parameter by five for each backtest. The optimiser would then use values 20,25,30,35,40,45,50,55 and 60.

Parameter	Range	Step
FastEMA	3 – 10	1
SlowEMA	20 – 60	5

Table 13.2 Strategy parameters, optimisation ranges and step increments

Once the parameter ranges are chosen, a data series (or bar period) and time frame can be selected. These are entered into the optimiser in the way they are selected in the backtest.

The optimiser has an additional section to enable the developer to select how many of the best optimised results to keep (ten by default) and what metric to optimise the strategy against.

The choices for the optimisation metric include:

- Maximum percent profitable (overall, long trades only, short trades only).

- Maximum average profit (overall, long trades only, short trades only).

- Maximum net profit (overall, long trades only, short trades only).

- Maximum profit factor (overall, long trades only, short trades only).

- Maximum win/loss ratio (overall, long trades only, short trades only).

- Minimum drawdown (overall, long trades only, short trades only).

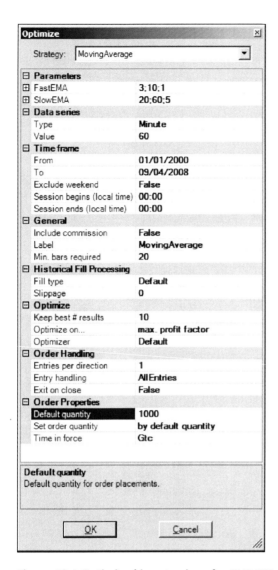

Figure 13.1 Optimised input values for EURJPY

Once OK is selected, the optimiser will perform a backtest against EURJPY for the chosen bar period and time frame for every single combination of parameters. For example, table 13.3 displays the first 15 backtest input parameters.

Backtest	Parameters (FastEMA, SlowEMA)
1	3, 20
2	4, 20
3	5, 20
4	6, 20
5	7, 20
6	8, 20
7	9, 20
8	10, 10
9	3, 25
10	4, 25
11	5, 25
12	6, 25
13	7, 25
14	8, 25
15	9, 25

Table 13.3 The first 15 iterations of an optimisation process

The process continues until every combination of both FastEMA and SlowEMA has been exhausted. It is therefore possible to understand that for a strategy that has many parameters, performing a full optimisation for multiple instruments and multiple time frames can take a considerably long time! Fortunately we are relying on computing power to perform this process. The manual equivalent would take weeks or months.

Figure 13.2 shows the top ten results of the optimisation process. The top result has the highest profit factor – which was our chosen performance metric. It is possible to observe that with our optimum parameters, the strategy did not return the highest net profit, the lowest drawdown, or lowest average MAE. It did, however, have the highest Sharpe ratio and highest percent profitable trades.

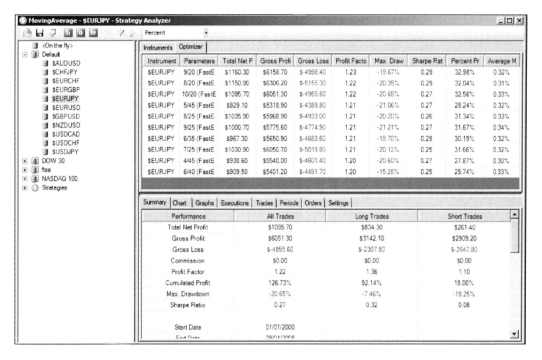

Figure 13.2 Moving average optimised results for EURJPY

The optimiser has chosen the optimum parameters for FastEMA and SlowEMA for this instrument, bar period (hourly charts) and time frame (between 1 April 2000 and 1 January 2007) to be 9 and 20 respectively. We can see this because these parameters are at the top of the list. From experience, I would suggest a re-run of the optimisation process using a slightly different parameter range because I would like to see the final parameters in the middle of my chosen range.

We can see that a FastEMA value of 9 is close to the highest value specified for that range of 3 to 10. We also observe that the SlowEMA value of 20 is right at the bottom of the SlowEMA range of 20 to 60. The second round of optimisation could possible use the ranges; SlowEMA (3;15;1) and FastEMA (16;24;1). Notice that the range for SlowEMA has been shortened and the increment reduced to 1.

Executing the optimisation process for the second time with the new parameter range provides a new set of performance metrics, and the final optimised parameters of 9 and 22 for FastEMA and SlowEMA respectively.

Instrument	FastMA	SlowMA	Total Net Profit	Profit Factor	Max. Drawdown	Sharpe Ratio	Percent Profitable	Average MAE
EURJPY	9	22	1,149.70	1.24	(20.27%)	0.29	32.65%	0.33%

Table 13.4 Final optimised metrics from EURJPY optimisation

Choosing a single set of optimised parameters for a whole basket of instruments is somewhat of a compromise as the final parameters chosen will not be ideal for all of the instruments based on our historic data. It should be remembered that we are not trying to perform our future long term trading based on previous curve fit parameters. We are actually trying to create a generalised strategy and parameter set that performs well for a range of instruments.

Many different processes exist for selecting the optimised parameters. Here are the two I use most regularly, in reverse order.

Option 1

If I only intend the system to run very short-term, perhaps less than three months, or I feel that the system is incomplete and I know that I have several changes and plenty of test cycles ahead, I will often optimise the strategy on the previous 12 month's worth of historic data only.

Certainly in the forex markets I have noticed that many short-term patterns tend to repeat frequently, but then fade out over time. By performing a short-term optimisation, and running the optimised parameters specific to each instrument, rather than a generalised set for the whole basket, I hope to achieve short-term gains. Whilst this strategy is not recommended for long term success it can be profitable in the very short-term.

Choosing this optimisation option requires frequent system changes to be made which goes against one of the major principles of creating a robust, long-term strategy.

When developing and optimising any strategy, the system developer will go through many cycles of strategy changes and testing. It is very important to document each cycle and keep a record of what was changed and how the change influenced the performance metrics observed. Regular reviews of these changes/metrics will clearly show the direction your strategy is heading in.

Instrument	FastEMA	SlowMA
AUDUSD	6	20
CHFJPY	7	24
EURCHF	12	26
EURGBP	6	22
EURJPY	8	24
EURUSD	9	20
GBPUSD	7	24
NZDUSD	12	26
USDCAD	12	26
USDCHF	3	20
USDJPY	12	22

Table 13.5 A set of optimisation results for a basket of instruments

From an optimisation we obtained the example optimum parameters in table 13.5. Notice how the optimiser produces different parameters for each instrument, and not a single set of parameters that work well for every instrument. Our challenge here is to do just that. My first step would be to re-run the optimisation process for the previous 6 or 12 months. Doing so would produce a new set of curve fit parameters individual to each instrument. Should any metrics obtained be unfavourable, ie, where no parameters were able to produce a profitable result, or if the optimum parameters were at the boundary edge, then I would widen the ranges to allow the optimiser more parameters to choose from.

After a final set of parameters is chosen for each instrument, I would trade the strategy with those specific parameters for a period of no longer than three months.

Option 2

Use an arithmetic function to select the parameters based on mean, median or mode.

- The mean, or average, is found by adding all of the results together and dividing the total by the number of results.

- The median is the middle value in the list after sorting the list into increasing order.

- The mode in a list of numbers refers to the numbers that occur most frequently.

Based on our previous optimised results:

Instrument	FastEMA	SlowEMA
AUDUSD	6	20
CHFJPY	7	24
EURCHF	12	26
EURGBP	6	22
EURJPY	8	24
EURUSD	9	20
GBPUSD	7	24
NZDUSD	12	26
USDCAD	12	26
USDCHF	3	20
USDJPY	12	22
Mean	**9**	**23**
Median	**8**	**24**
Mode	**12**	**20**

Table 13.6 The arithmetic mean, median and mode of the optimised parameters

After calculating the mean, median and mode, we now have reduced the different combinations of parameters down to only three. Further backtesting can now be performed on all three to find the single combination that produces the best performance metrics.

14

Strategy Development – Putting It All Together

Strategy Introduction

The aim of this chapter is to take all of the different components of a strategy discussed so far and combine them to create an idea for a strategy, develop the idea using the NinjaTrader strategy wizard, and then backtest and optimise the strategy to end up with a trading system ready for further testing and detailed analysis.

We will create a strategy that captures the swing movement of an instrument that oscillates above and below a long term moving average. When the price action moves above the long-term average we will enter a long position. A short entry will occur when the price action moves below the long-term average.

Two short duration exponential moving averages will be used to exit the trade when these moving averages crossover.

The long term moving average will actually be two moving averages, one based on the high price, one based on the low, this forms a high/low price channel. These moving averages will also act as the stops. For example, when the price action moves through the MA of the high, a long position will be opened. Should the price move down below the MA of the high and back into the channel we consider the trade to have gone against us and an exit is triggered. Basing the stops on a moving average allows more flexibility in the trade, but means that the stop size can vary for each trade.

Figure 14.1 Demonstrates a trade either side of our price channel

Figure 14.1 shows two complete trades using the strategy. The first trade is a short trade entered as the price action broke below the low of the channel. The trade exited when the short period EMAs crossed. The second trade is a long position entered when the price action crossed above the high of the channel. The position was closed when the EMAs crossed.

Strategy High Level Definition

The following steps are a high-level description of how the strategy will function.

1. Create a channel based on a long duration moving average of the high and low prices.

2. Go long if the close price breaks out above the channel.

3. Go short if the close price breaks below the channel.

4. Have two shorter duration moving averages to close the positions as the price reverses back towards the channel.

5. Have an additional technical close for a situation where the price action closes back inside the channel before the shorter duration MAs trigger.

Strategy Formula Definition

Our open and close criteria can be defined as:

Position Trigger	Formula	Description
Open Long	If Close[0] crosses above SMA(High, ChannelPeriod)	If the close value of the current bar crosses above the long period simple moving average of the highs, then open a long position
Close Long	If EMA(FastEMA[0]) crosses below EMA(SlowEMA[0])	If the FastEMA of the current bar crosses below the SlowEMA of the current bar, then close the long position
Open Short	If Close[0] crosses below SMA(Low, ChannelPeriod)	If the close value of the current bar crosses below the long period simple moving average of the lows, then open a short position
Close Short	If EMA(FastEMA[0]) crosses above EMA(SlowEMA[0])	If the FastEMA of the current bar crosses above the SlowEMA of the current bar, then close the short position

Table 14.1 Trade entry criteria for the channel crossover strategy

In addition to the above criteria, we will also try to minimise the damage caused by whipsaws. This can be done by closing open positions if the price action goes against us before the EMA crossover has occurred.

Position Trigger	Formula	Description
Close Long	If Close[0] < SMA(High, ChannelPeriod)	If the close value of the current bar is less than the long period simple moving average (ie, the price has moved back inside the channel), then close the long position
Close Short	If Close[0] > SMA(Low, ChannelPeriod)	If the close value of the current bar is greater than the long period simple moving average (ie, the price has moved back inside the channel), then close the short position

Table 14.2 Exit criteria for the channel crossover strategy

When creating a strategy be sure to understand the difference between crosses above and greater than. The crosses above operator should be used when you wish the condition to be true when the indicator or price action (expressed on the left hand side of the formula) actually crosses above a second price or indicator (expressed on the left hand side of the formula). The strategy wizard allows you to define in what bar period the condition occurred, so for example you could specify that the price action has crossed an indicator within the last five bars. The greater than operator is purely for when the value of one expression is larger than the value of the second expression. It has no concept of whether the value was previously less than or equal to.

Strategy Creation

Now that we have defined our strategy in mathematical terms, it is possible to use the strategy wizard to create the strategy. This section presents a step-by-step guide to creating our strategy using NinjaTrader.

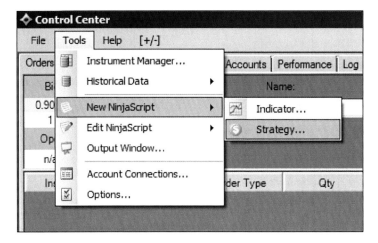

Figure 14.2 Locating the Strategy Wizard within NinjaTrader

From within NinjaTrader, select Tools -> New NinjaScript -> Strategy

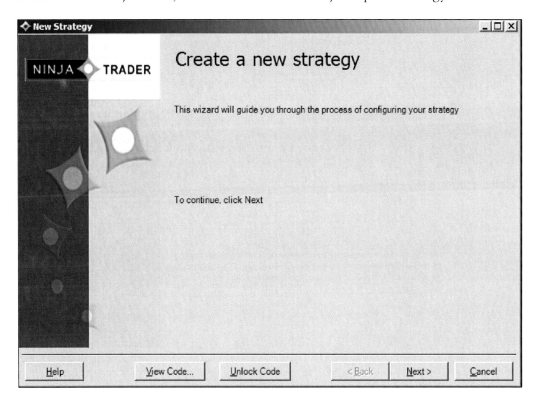

Figure 14.3 The strategy wizard initial splash screen

On the initial strategy creation screen, select Next to continue.

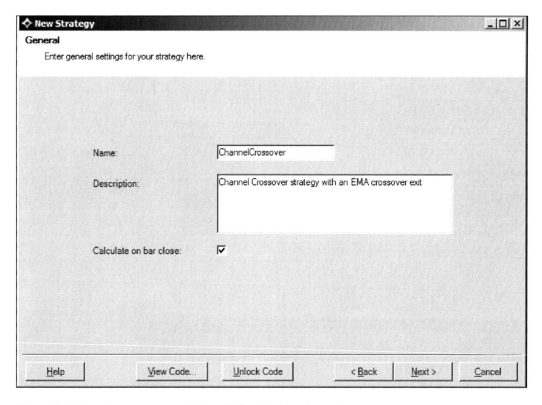

Figure 14.4 Entering a name and description for the channel crossover strategy

Enter a unique name for the strategy and a description, and select Next.

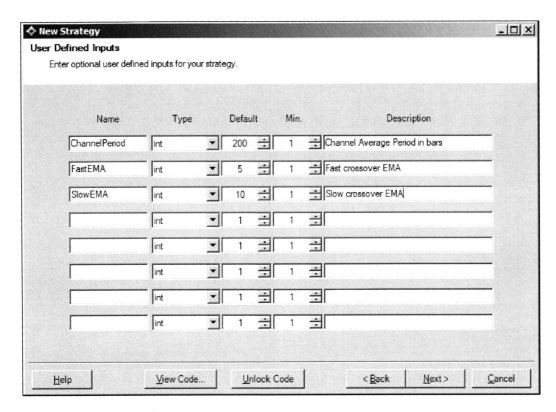

Figure 14.5 Specifying the parameters to use for the channel crossover strategy

At this stage we define our three input parameters and assign them with default values, and select Next.

Parameter	Description
ChannelPeriod	This is the long duration moving average value that will be used to define the channel for the price action to move out of. Use a default value of 200 during strategy creation. This can be changed later if required.
FastEMA	A very short duration moving average value to be used in conjunction with the SlowEMA to exit the position. Use a default value of 5 during strategy creation. This can be changed later if required.
SlowEMA	Another short duration (although slightly longer than the FastEMA) moving average. Use a default value of 10 during strategy creation This can be changed later if required.

Table 14.3 A description of the parameters used in the channel crossover strategy

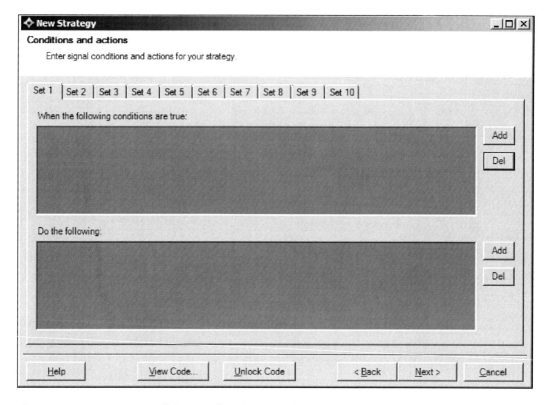

Figure 14.6 An empty Conditions and Actions window

The conditions and actions window has a series of ten tabs. Each tab represents a conditional formula for our strategy. The conditions are displayed in the upper pane, and their corresponding actions are displayed in the lower pane. Conditions are added and deleted using the Add and Del buttons, respectively, at the right hand side of the window.

All of the conditions within a single conditions pane are combined using a logical AND function, ie, if all of the conditions are true the action in the Action pane is performed.

All of the sets are combined using a logical OR function, ie, any one of the sets can function independently.

To create our first condition, select the upper Add button, and the condition builder window appears.

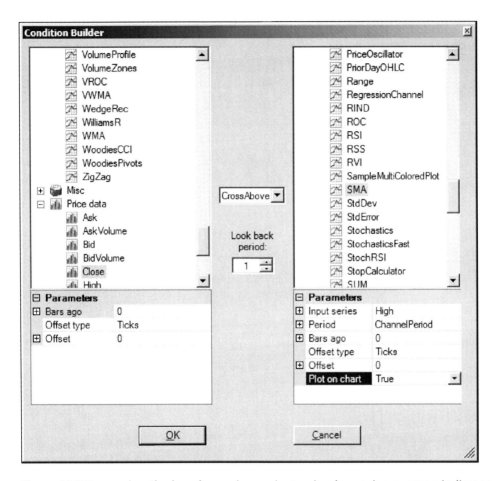

Figure 14.7 Comparing the bar close price against a simple moving average indicator

Figure 14.7 is created by scrolling down in the left hand pane until the Price data section is reached. Expand the section and select Close. The parameter values then appear in the bottom left pane. Leave these as the default values.

Change the drop down list in the centre of the condition builder window to be CrossAbove.

In the right hand pane, in the Indicators section, scroll down and select EMA. In the Parameters section, change the Period value to be our ChannelPeriod parameter by selecting the Period box where the value 14 is displayed. A Value box appears and the ChannelPeriod parameter can be selected.

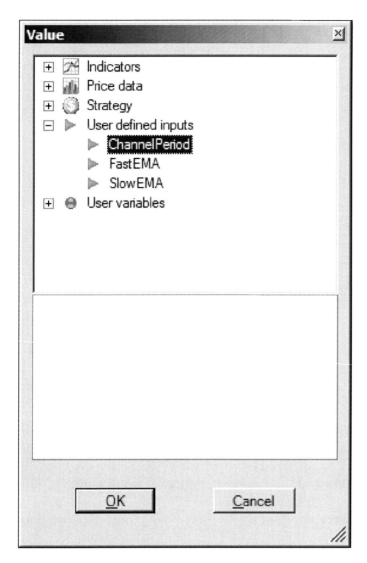

Figure 14.8 Selecting the ChannelPeriod parameter

Change the Plot on chart value to True, as we wish to be able to see the channel plotted on our charts during backtesting and real-time execution.

We also need to change the Input Series value to represent the High values. In the right hand parameters section, click on DefaultInput, and select High from the Price data section.

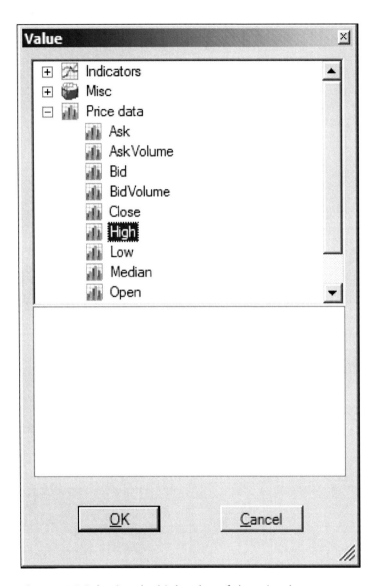

Figure 14.9 Selecting the high value of the price data

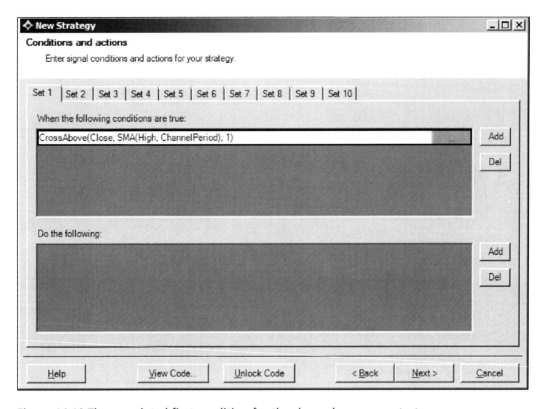

Figure 14.10 The completed first condition for the channel crossover strategy

In order to create our order entry we need to add an action for the condition. Select the Add button for the bottom pane.

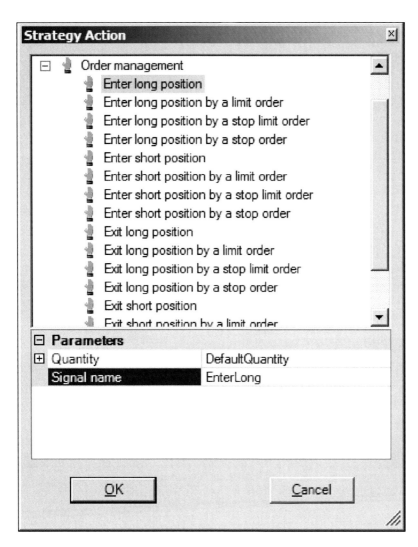

Figure 14.11 Defining a long entry action

This action enters a long market order, with a signal name of EnterLong.

The resultant condition and action for the first tab in the condition builder is shown in figure 14.12.

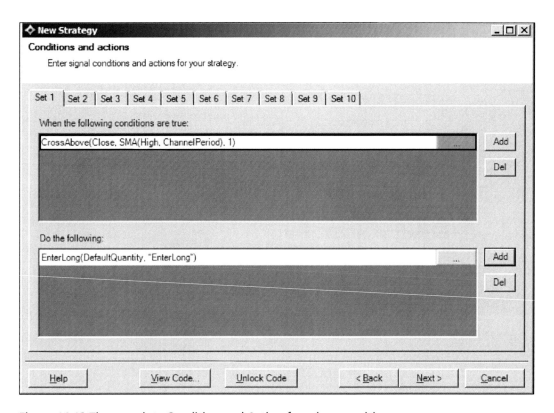

Figure 14.12 The complete Condition and Action for a long position

The following screenshots show the completed conditions and actions for the remaining tabs.

Set 2 Tab

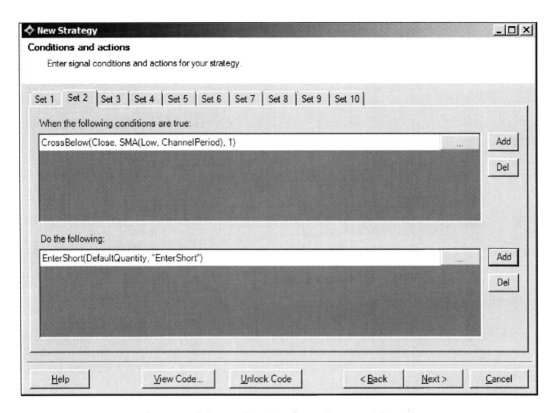

Figure 14.13 The complete Condition and Action for a short position

Set 3 Tab

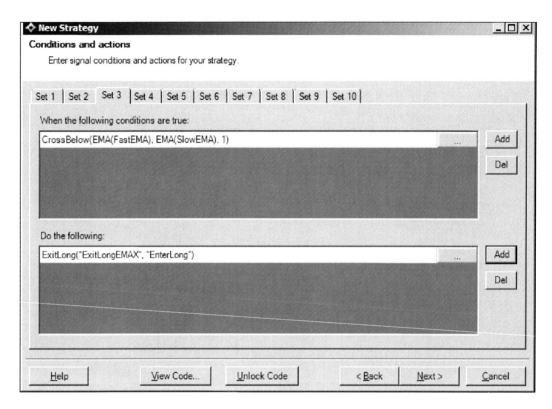

Figure 14.14 The complete Condition and Action to exit a long position

Set 4 Tab

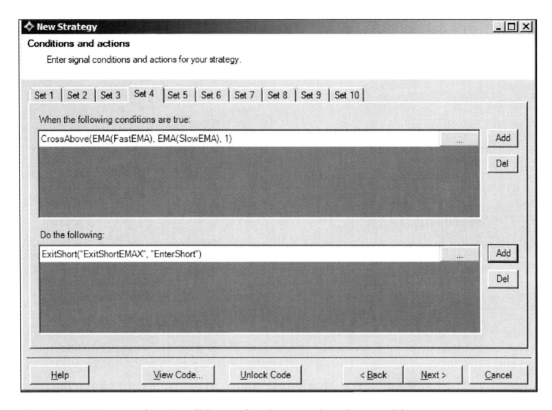

Figure 14.15 The complete Condition and Action to exit a short position

Set 5 Tab

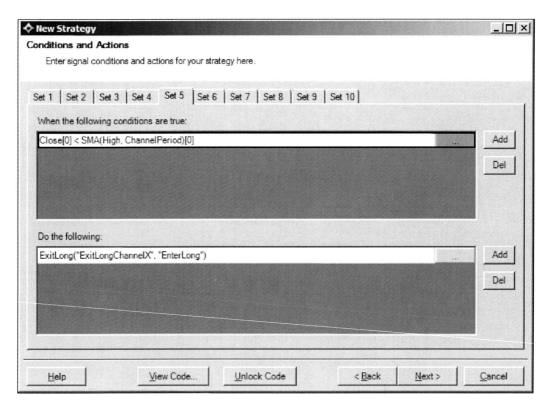

Figure 14.16 The complete Condition and Action to exit a long position

Set 6 Tab

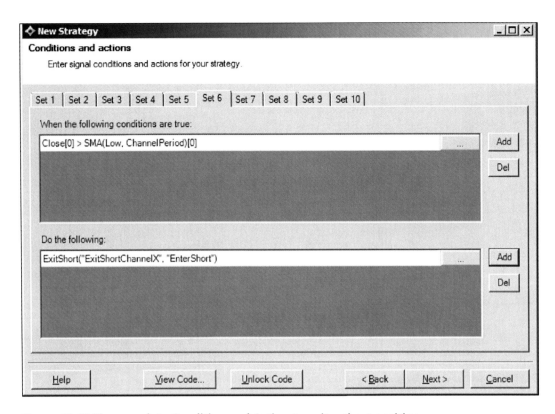

Figure 14.17 The complete Condition and Action to exit a short position

When all of the conditions and actions for the six tabs have been entered, select Next.

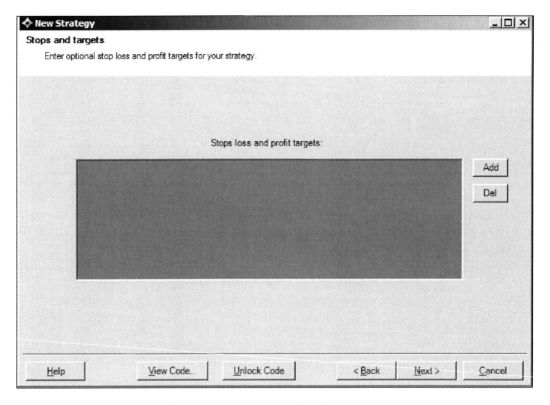

Figure 14.18 No stops or profit targets are to be defined

Leave the stops and targets section blank, and select Next.

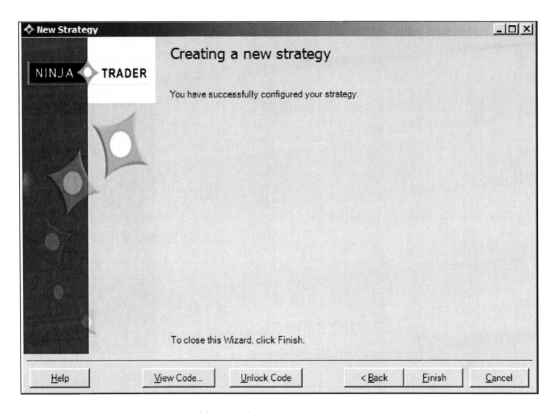

Figure 14.19 The strategy wizard is complete

A final click on Finish and the strategy should be created successfully.

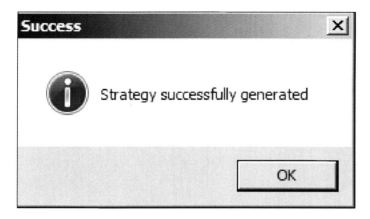

Figure 14.20 The strategy has now been compiled and is available in NinjaTrader

Strategy Testing

Now that the strategy has been created, we need to run a quick test to make sure that our entry and exit conditions are being filled correctly.

Before performing the backtest, ensure that you are connected to your historic data feed. If you have previously installed a series of historic data no connection is required.

Open a Strategy Analyzer window.

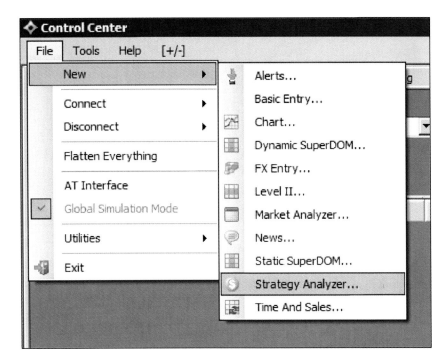

Figure 14.21 Locating the Strategy Analyzer in NinjaTrader

Figure 14.22 shows the default Strategy Analyser window before any backtesting has been performed. During system development, the performance outputs displayed in this window are very important to ensure that the system you are developing is not only profitable but also tradable.

At the top of the Strategy Analyzer window, in the middle, there exists a drop down list that allows you to select from three options: Currency, Percent and Points. When performing backtesting I personally prefer to have Percent or Points selected, as the Currency values are highly dependent on the position size and the initial account size, which, at this stage of backtesting, I am not really interested in.

In later chapters we will export the Points data created during a backtest and perform detailed analysis on the results using a position sizing technique.

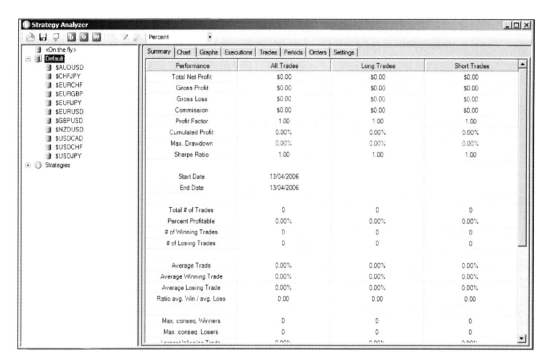

Figure 14.22 The Strategy Analyzer window before a backtest has been performed

Select an instrument from the left hand pane. In this example I will use $GBPUSD and select the backtest button.

When the backtest window appears, select the Channel Crossing strategy, and modify all of the input values to match the historic data installed on your system.

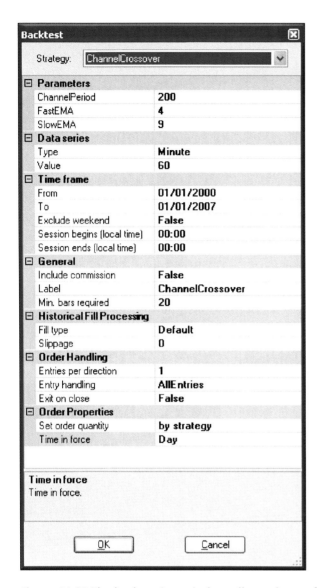

Figure 14.23 The backtesting window allows the configuration of backtest parameters

Selecting OK will execute the backtest. Ignore all of the data on the Summary tab, and select the Chart tab. We need to check that each of six conditions is being met correctly.

Condition	Position Trigger	Formula
1	Open Long	If Close[0] crosses above SMA(High, 200)
2	Close Long	If EMA(FastEMA[0]) crosses below EMA(SlowEMA[0])
3	Open Short	If Close[0] crosses below SMA(Low, 200)
4	Close Short	If EMA(FastEMA[0]) crosses above EMA(SlowEMA[0])
5	Close Long	If Close[0] < SMA(High, 200)
6	Close Short	If Close[0] > SMA(Low, 200)

Table 14.4 The six formulas used in the Channel Crossing strategy

Figure 14.24 Long position entry and exit

Figure 14.24 shows the entry and exit criteria for a long trade. The entry occurs when the closing price of the bar has crossed above the high of the long period moving average. The backtest has been performed with the CalculateOnBar Close setting as True, hence the position is opened on the bar after our trigger bar. The Strategy Analyzer has labelled the entry condition as EnterLong, which is the label chosen when we created the strategy. The quantity and price are also displayed next to the entry label.

The position exit occurred when the two moving averages crossed over. As before, with CalculateOnBar Close set to true, the actual closing price is the open price of the following bar. The trade exit has been labelled as ExitLongEMAX, which is our description for a long exit based on EMA crossover.

Figure 14.25 Short position entry and exit

Figure 14.25 shows the entry and exit criteria for a short trade. The entry occurs when the closing price of the bar crosses below the low of the long period moving average. The backtest has been performed with the CalculateOnBar Close setting as True, hence the position is opened on the bar after our trigger bar. The Strategy Analyzer has labelled the entry condition as EnterShort.

The exit occurred when the two moving averages crossed over. As before, with CalculateOnBar Close set to true, the actual closing price is the open price of the following bar. The trade exit has been labelled as ExitShortEMAX.

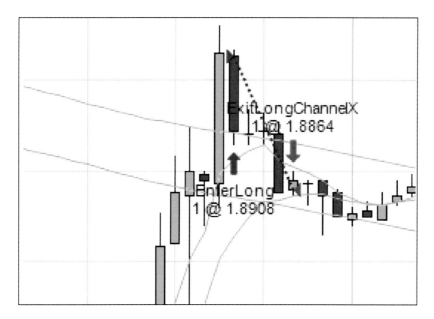

Figure 14.26 Long position exit

Figure 14.26 shows the exit of a Long position where the trade has gone against us. We can see that on the entry bar the price went against us and three bars later the price had closed within our channel, triggering one of our exit criteria. The position was then closed at the open of the following bar.

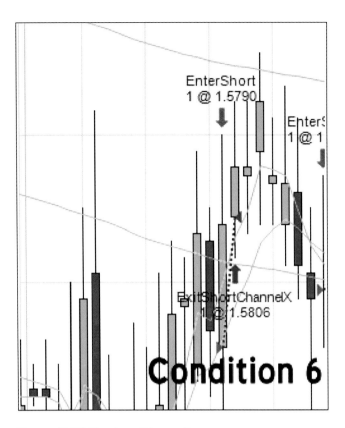

Figure 14.27 Short position exit

Figure 14.27 shows the exit of a Short position where the trade has gone against us. We can see immediately that the bar we opened the trade on closed within the channel triggering a close on the following bar.

The screenshots confirm that all of our 6 conditions are being filled correctly.

Simple backtest and analysis

Switching back to the Summary tab shows that whilst the performance statistics are quite poor, the strategy has been profitable based on the default parameters and the time period and instrument chosen.

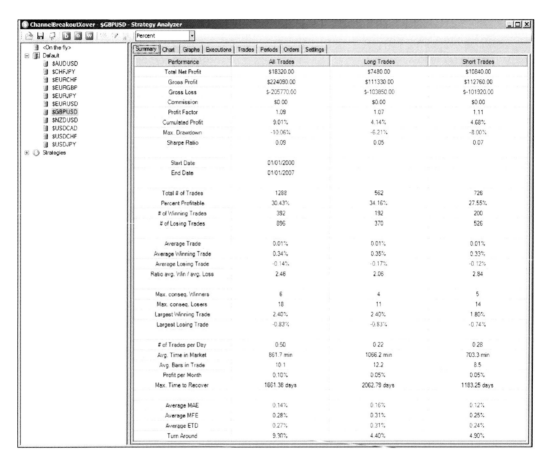

Figure 14.28 The summary tab gives an overall view of the metrics for the entire backtest

Instrument	Total Net Profit	Profit Factor	Max. Drawdown	Sharpe Ratio	Percent Profitable	Average MAE
GBPUSD	18,320	1.09	-10.06%	0.09	30.43%	0.14%

Table 14.5 The results for our primary focus performance metrics

Simple optimisation and analysis

We will now use the optimisation feature of NinjaTrader to curve fit a series of successful parameters for our strategy to the $GBPUSD instrument.

In the Strategy Analyzer window, select the optimise button.

Change the parameters and time frame as shown in table 14.6.

Parameter	Range	Step
ChannelPeriod	150-250	10
FastEMA	4 – 10	1
SlowEMA	8 – 20	2
Time Frame	1/1/2005 to 1/1/2007	n/a

Table 14.6 Detailing the parameter ranges and incremental step for each parameter

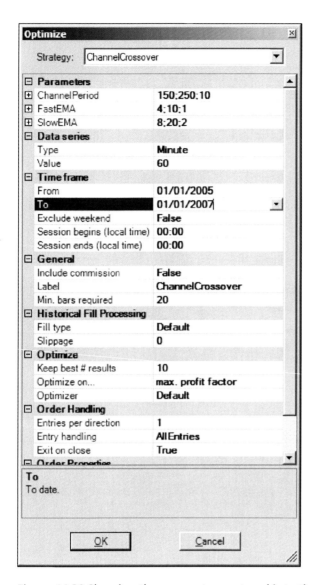

Figure 14.29 Showing the parameters entered into the optimisation backtest tool

Select OK to run the optimisation. The process will take sometime to complete depending on the speed of your PC.

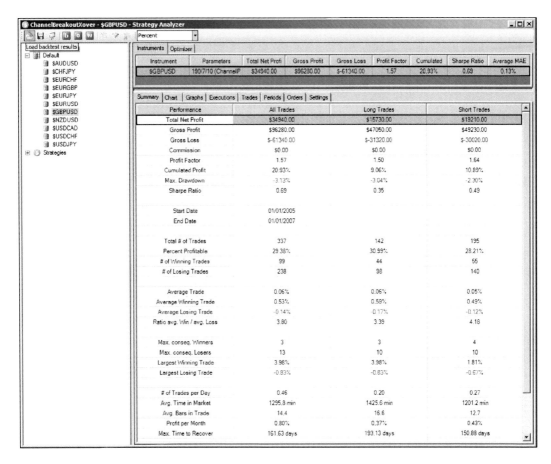

Figure 14.30 Showing the optimised parameter backtest results

What we have achieved here is the curve fitting of our strategy to our historic data for the time frame specified in the backtest and for the bar period of 60 minutes. The parameters produced by the strategy analyser are the optimum values to obtain the maximum profit factor.

Parameter	Value
ChannelPeriod	190
FastEMA	7
SlowEMA	10

Table 14.7 Details the optimum parameters for our instrument for the time period backtested

It is unlikely that these will be the final parameters used when we execute the system in real-time trading. If we were to re-run the backtest using a different time frame but keeping the instrument and bar period identical, it is highly likely that the optimiser will return slightly different values.

When I develop a trading system I aim to create a single strategy that works for a range of instruments using the same parameters. By doing this I hope to avoid curve fitting my strategy to my data, with the result that the more generalised strategy and parameters work well over various market conditions.

Full Basket Optimisation

We will now execute the same optimisation for a larger time frame and for all of our instruments. To do this select the high level folder that is your basket of instruments, and then select the Optimise button.

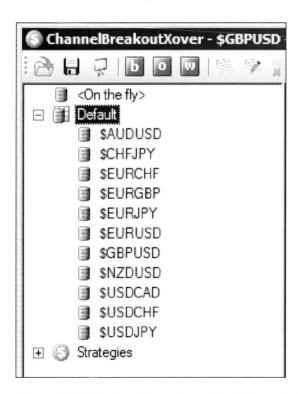

Figure 14.31 Selecting the entire backtest for optimisation

The optimiser window will appear containing the same range of parameters used for the last optimiser session. Leave these values, but just extend the time frame based on the historic data you have available. I will test the period 1 April 2000 to 1 January 2007 as I have data in this time period for all of the instruments in my basket. In addition, the parameter range for the EMAs has been widened.

Parameter	Range	Step
ChannelPeriod	150-250	10
FastEMA	2 – 10	1
SlowEMA	12 – 30	2
Time Frame	1/4/2000 to 1/1/2007	n/a

Table 14.8 Detailing the parameter ranges and incremental step for each parameter

Select OK. This time, the optimiser will take significantly longer to run.

It is often useful to save the performance results after a large optimisation run. The results can be saved by right clicking on the performance summary screen and selecting Save As or Export to Excel.

Once the optimisation session has completed, the Instruments tab displays the optimum parameters for each instrument. Note that it is unlikely that each instrument shares the same optimum parameters.

The Optimizer tab shows, in descending order, the top ten parameters used for each instrument ordered by success. The first set of parameters is the same as those given on the Instrument tab. The number of best results can be set before the optimisation process is executed. Ten is the default value.

Our task is to document the parameters and then, through process of deduction, choose a series of parameters to use for the entire basket of instruments.

Instrument	Channel	FastMA	SlowMA	Total Net Profit	Profit Factor	Max. Drawdown	Sharpe Ratio	Percent Profitable	Average MAE
AUDUSD	180	2	12	21,790	1.21	-8.07%	0.2	31.48%	0.20%
CHFJPY	190	4	14	18,850	1.15	-12.61%	0.14	30.45%	0.19%
EURCHF	200	5	28	-26,790	0.79	-19.88%	-0.29	29.20%	0.11%
EURGBP	250	6	28	15,530	1.21	-7.16%	0.23	27.33%	0.17%
EURJPY	210	2	20	48,790	1.29	-16.77%	0.24	28.26%	0.20%
EURUSD	170	3	18	50,030	1.32	-8.52%	0.37	28.04%	0.18%
GBPUSD	250	2	18	34,940	1.2	-8.19%	0.17	27.87%	0.15%
NZDUSD	150	9	14	-3820	0.97	-34.49%	-0.11	26.86%	0.26%
USDCAD	190	2	20	20,240	1.13	-8.70%	0.13	28.26%	0.14%
USDCHF	190	2	20	62,850	1.3	-4.88%	0.43	27.68%	0.19%
USDJPY	250	10	26	27,430	1.17	-14.61%	0.16	22.89%	0.19%

Table 14.9 Results of optimisation

Table 14.9 shows the optimised parameters and results. There are some interesting observations from the above optimisation:

- EURGBP has chosen the parameters at the maximum edge of the range (ChannelPeriod is 250) which suggests that further backtesting with a different range, perhaps 200-300, is needed to find the optimum parameters for this instrument.

- The optimiser was unable to find any parameters in our range that resulted in a profitable outcome for EURCHF or NZDUSD. This does not mean that the strategy will not work for those instruments, it just means that no optimum parameters exist for the entire time frame tested. If the optimisation process was repeated using a shorter time frame, then successful parameters would be found.

Statistic	Channel	FastMA	SlowMA
Mean	185	3	13
Median	190	3	20
Mode	190	2	20

Table 14.10 Details the optimum parameters for our instrument for the time period backtested

Once the parameters in table 14.10 have been obtained it is necessary to perform the backtest again using these three sets of parameters.

Instrument	Total Net Profit	Profit Factor	Max. Drawdown	Sharpe Ratio	Percent Profitable	Average MAE
AUDUSD	12,610	1.11	-11.53%	0.09	28.43%	0.21%
CHFJPY	14,990	1.13	-12.11%	0.11	30.38%	0.19%
EURCHF	-45,150	0.65	-26.72%	-0.61	31.38%	0.11%
EURGBP	-7790	0.91	-23.75%	-0.13	30.27%	0.16%
EURJPY	40,860	1.24	-15.15%	0.21	28.90%	0.19%
EURUSD	37,490	1.25	-7.35%	0.24	28.51%	0.17%
GBPUSD	20,480	1.1	-8.05%	0.1	27.21%	0.15%
NZDUSD	-20,900	0.84	-35.52%	-0.25	27.93%	0.25%
USDCAD	620	1	-11.61%	-0.02	29.62%	0.14%
USDCHF	40,830	1.19	-4.52%	0.28	27.70%	0.18%
USDJPY	350	1	-15.15%	-0.01	27.05%	0.17%
Totals	**94,390**	**1.04**	**-35.52%**	**0.00**	**28.85%**	**0.17%**

Table 14.11 Results of backtest with mean parameters (185, 3, 13)

Explanation of the totals row:

Total Net Profit: This is the gross value of all of the instruments summed together to provide an overall profit figure for the backtest.

Profit Factor: This is the average profit factor metric for all of the instruments.

Maximum Drawdown: This is the highest individual drawdown figure for all of the instruments.

Sharpe Ratio: This is the average Sharpe ratio for all of the instruments.

Percentage Profitable: This is the average percentage profitable figure.

Average MAE: This is the average of all of the average MAEs for the backtest.

Instrument	Total Net Profit	Profit Factor	Max. Drawdown	Sharpe Ratio	Percent Profitable	Average MAE
AUDUSD	7,560	1.06	-13.29%	0.06	25.24%	0.22%
CHFJPY	11,070	1.09	-13.63%	0.08	29.07%	0.19%
EURCHF	-39,870	0.7	-24.58%	-0.45	29.93%	0.11%
EURGBP	-3,570	0.96	-18.53%	-0.06	28.10%	0.16%
EURJPY	39,140	1.22	-15.46%	0.2	27.74%	0.20%
EURUSD	35,810	1.23	-8.61%	0.24	26.77%	0.18%
GBPUSD	16,130	1.07	-12.60%	0.06	25.30%	0.15%
NZDUSD	-18,110	0.86	-33.83%	-0.22	26.34%	0.25%
USDCAD	14,980	1.1	-11.51%	0.08	27.68%	0.15%
USDCHF	60,060	1.28	-3.70%	0.4	26.37%	0.19%
USDJPY	-5,170	0.97	-17.46%	-0.05	24.70%	0.18%
Total/Average	**118,030**	**1.05**	**-33.83%**	**0.03**	**27.02%**	**0.18%**

Table 14.12 Results of backtest with median parameters (190, 3, 20)

Instrument	Total Net Profit	Profit Factor	Max. Drawdown	Sharpe Ratio	Percent Profitable	Average MAE
AUDUSD	8690	1.08	-11.23%	0.06	26.53%	0.21%
CHFJPY	15,200	1.13	-11.24%	0.11	30.45%	0.19%
EURCHF	-42,050	0.67	-24.87%	-0.52	30.34%	0.11%
EURGBP	-3,240	0.96	-18.34%	-0.06	28.87%	0.16%
EURJPY	45,380	1.26	-14.58%	0.24	29.37%	0.19%
EURUSD	37,360	1.25	-6.87%	0.25	27.68%	0.18%
GBPUSD	23,980	1.11	-12.31%	0.1	26.58%	0.15%
NZDUSD	-19,710	0.85	-33.92%	-0.25	26.81%	0.25%
USDCAD	20,240	1.13	-8.70%	0.13	28.26%	0.14%
USDCHF	62,850	1.3	-4.88%	0.43	27.68%	0.19%
USDJPY	-7940	0.95	-18.04%	-0.06	25.50%	0.17%
Total/Average	**140,760**	**1.06**	**-33.92%**	**0.04**	**28.00%**	**0.17%**

Table 14.13 Results of backtest with mode parameters (190,2,20)

Statistic	Parameters	Total Net Profit	Avg. Profit Factor	Highest Max. Drawdown	Avg. Sharpe Ratio	Avg. Percent Profitable	Avg. Average MAE
Mean	185,3,13	94,390	1.04	-35.52%	0.00	28.85%	0.17%
Median	190,3,20	118,030	1.05	-33.83%	0.03	27.02%	0.18%
Mode	190,2,20	140,760	1.06	-33.92%	0.04	28.00%	0.17%

Table 14.14 Overall results for the three different backtests of mean, median and mode

We can see from table 14.14 that the parameters chosen by taking the statistical mode of the optimised parameters produces the best result.

It is important to remember that all of the metrics generated in these backtests have been for a single time frame. It is also necessary to perform backtesting for multiple time frames.

These backtests have also been performed without factoring in commission or slippage and no money management rules have been applied. These can be applied during the detailed results analysis on the out of sample backtest.

Full Basket out of sample backtest

An out of sample backtest for the period 1 January 2007 to 1 January 2008 using our parameters (190,2,20) produces the results in table 14.15.

Instrument	Total Net Profit	Profit Factor	Max. Drawdown	Sharpe Ratio	Percent Profitable	Average MAE
AUDUSD	14,980	2.36	-2.58%	0.84	36.51%	0.19%
CHFJPY	-8,420	0.68	-10.55%	-0.52	22.78%	0.16%
EURCHF	6,550	1.6	-0.83%	0.78	38.73%	0.07%
EURGBP	3,440	1.51	-1.45%	0.74	30.85%	0.09%
EURJPY	7,320	1.26	-3.53%	0.38	26.63%	0.16%
EURUSD	3,700	1.24	-2.21%	0.24	26.85%	0.12%
GBPUSD	8,830	1.39	-1.88%	0.5	29.14%	0.13%
NZDUSD	14,430	1.7	-4.27%	0.72	22.94%	0.45%
USDCAD	-2,850	0.87	-4.86%	-0.17	26.32%	0.18%
USDCHF	7,220	1.57	-2.14%	0.48	28.38%	0.11%
USDJPY	7,770	1.42	-4.86%	0.43	27.93%	0.15%

Table 14.15 Results of out of sample backtest using optimised parameters

Summary And Future Enhancement

The out of sample backtest has displayed a profitable system for the previous year, but the values do not take into account any commission, slippage or money management techniques.

Looking at the charts of the trades, an example of which is shown in figure 14.32, it is possible to see that the system is affected by whipsaws. It is also possible to tell this by the Percentage Profitable metric, which has a similar hit rate to a typical trend following system.

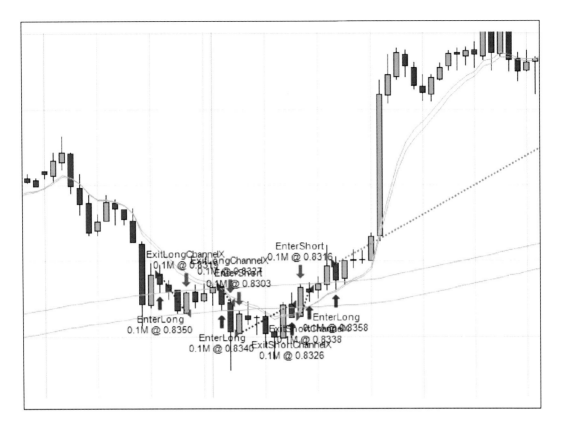

Figure 14.32 Several whipsaw trades

It is possible to reduce the number of whipsaws by adding a filter to the entry criteria. Possible filters include:

- Have a filter based on Average True Range to reduce the trade entry on high volatility bars. An example could be to check if ATR(1) [0] < 1.5 * ATR(10) [0]. This formula checks to see if the volatility of the current bar is less than 1.5 times the average volatility of the ten previous bars.

- Use ADX and DMI to see if the instrument is trending with a bullish trend. For example, before opening a long position, check that ADX > 20 and that DMI+ is greater than DMI-.

Other changes to the general strategy may include:

- Change the EMAs to close a position to be FastEMA(high), SlowEMA(high) for long closes, and FastEMA(low), SlowEMA(low) for short closes.

- Check the correlation between instruments frequently, and only trade the non-correlated, or positively correlated ones. Ignore the instruments that are negatively correlated as the profits and losses may be cancelled out.

- Develop and backtest different exit strategies. This strategy only uses a simple exit. Multiple exit strategies based on the volatility of the instrument, how the trade is progressing and probability of trade success should also be examined.

- The strategy does not have any fixed stop values, but you can still place stops when you open a trade. Just calculate the distance between the trade opening price and the closest edge of the channel. This is your stop size because if the price went beyond this point the strategy would exit on bar close. Ideally this would be coded into the strategy, but it is not possible to do this calculation using the NinjaTrader strategy wizard. It is possible with NinjaScript though.

- Adjust the strategy in NinjaScript so that the stop is the distance between current price and the other side of the channel, ie, if short then stop size = current price – (SMA(190),High), hence position size = INT(Account Capital * 0.01)/stop size.

- Have a channel multiplication factor (x * high, x * low) so that the width of the channel can vary as a parameter.

- Check that the previous X bars opened and closed within the channel.

- You could modify the channel so that it is based on Donchian bands, or Bollinger bands.

- Change the exits so that it is the channel edge on the opposite side to close the trade. This creates a wider stop, but allows the position freedom to move.

- Maybe have several entries per direction.

- Prevent a trade reversal, thus stopping a position immediately going from one direction to the opposite direction on the same bar.

15

Detailed Results Analysis

To perform further analysis on the results of our out-of-sample backtest in the previous chapter, we must export details of each trade into Microsoft Excel. From the Strategy Analyzer window, select one of the instrument rows from the previous backtest (in this example we will use $AUDUSD) that shows the backtest summary, and then select the Trades tab. For spread betting, we are directly interested in the number of points gained or lost on each trade, so make sure the drop down list at the top of the window is set to Points.

Right click on the part of the window displaying all of the trades and a short menu will appear. Select Export to Excel. Assuming that Microsoft Excel is installed, NinjaTrader opens Excel with the trade data. At this point it is usually a good idea to save the data. My personal preference is to save it as an .xls file rather than .csv as all of the formatting is retained.

Locate the Profit column in the Excel spreadsheet. It is important that this column represents the number of points won or lost for the trade. Depending on the position size used in the Default Quantity box when running the strategy, the value in this Excel column may be a multiple of the number of points. For example, taking the first line in my Excel spreadsheet shown in table 15.1.

Entry Price	Exit Price	Profit
0.7938	0.7945	-70.0000

Table 15.1 Extracting points data from the trade results

I can see that the difference between the Entry and Exit price is seven tics, and the profit is -70. So the profit value is ten times higher than the number of tics lost in this trade. This means that all of the values in my profit column are a factor of ten out. At this point you could re-run the backtest using a smaller position size, perhaps using a default quantity of 1,000 rather than 10,000. But the easiest thing to do is create an additional column (called Points) to the right of the Profit column in the spreadsheet. Then create a formula to divide all of the values in the Profit column by ten and put them in the Points column.

Ie, if Column M is the Profit column, then in cell N1 would be the label Points, and cell N2 would be the formula "=M2/10". This formula would then need to be copied down the rest of the Points column. A quick way of doing this is to select the N2 cell, hold down shift, and then double click on the bottom right corner of the N2 cell.

Typically for most currency pairs with a tick size of 0.0001 (ie, GBPUSB, EURUSD etc) you will divide the profit column by ten assuming that you used a default position size of 100,000. For currency pairs with a tick size of 0.01 (ie, EURJPY, CHFJPY) you will need to divide the profit column by 1,000.

Now add another column to the right hand side of Points, and call this column Actual Profit. Fill this column with the formula of "=N2-6", ie, Points column minus a static slippage value of six. In this example I will calculate my slippage as being six points, this includes the three points spread set by the spread betting company for this instrument, and a further three points lost whilst I placed the trade. You may decide not to include the latter, as sometime this slippage works in your favour, so it is possible that over time it will balance out to zero.

From analysis of the metrics produced in the out of sample backtest for the Channel Crossover strategy it is possible to determine that the Average Maximum Adverse Excursion for all of the instruments is 183 points. This value will be used in conjunction with our risk size to create a position size per point.

Add a further column to the right hand side of Actual Profit, but rather than entering a title for the column enter the value 100,000. Then in the cell below, P2, enter the formula:

=P1+(INT((P1*0.01)/183)*O2)

(Where Cell O2 is the first numeric value in the Actual Profit column).

Copy the formula in P2 down the entire column to the last trade.

We have used a value of 100,000 to represent an initial account value of £100K.

We also place each trade at 1% of account size, with the initial trade being approximately £5 per point. The strategy we are backtesting does not have a fixed stop-loss value, so using our previous money management technique we calculate a position size to limit a losing trade to be no more than 1% of account capital based on an Average MAE of 183 points.

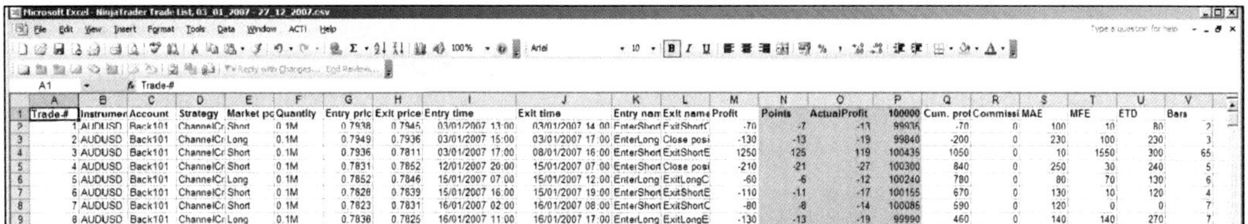

Trade-#	Instrumen	Account	Strategy	Market pc	Quantity	Entry pric	Exit price	Entry time	Exit time	Entry nam	Exit name	Profit	Points	ActualProfit	100000	Cum. prof	Commissi	MAE	MFE	ETD	Bars
1	AUDUSD	Back101	ChannelCr	Short	0.1M	0.7938	0.7945	03/01/2007 13:00	03/01/2007 14:00	EnterShort	ExitShortC	-70	-7	-13	99936	-70	0	100	10	80	2
2	AUDUSD	Back101	ChannelCr	Long	0.1M	0.7949	0.7936	03/01/2007 15:00	03/01/2007 17:00	EnterLong	Close posi	-130	-13	-19	99840	-200	0	230	100	230	3
3	AUDUSD	Back101	ChannelCr	Short	0.1M	0.7936	0.7811	03/01/2007 17:00	08/01/2007 16:00	EnterShort	ExitShortE	1250	125	119	100435	1050	0	10	1550	300	65
4	AUDUSD	Back101	ChannelCr	Short	0.1M	0.7831	0.7852	12/01/2007 20:00	15/01/2007 07:00	EnterShort	Close posi	-210	-21	-27	100300	840	0	250	30	240	5
5	AUDUSD	Back101	ChannelCr	Long	0.1M	0.7852	0.7846	15/01/2007 07:00	15/01/2007 12:00	EnterLong	ExitLongC	-60	-6	-12	100240	780	0	80	70	130	6
6	AUDUSD	Back101	ChannelCr	Short	0.1M	0.7828	0.7839	15/01/2007 16:00	15/01/2007 19:00	EnterShort	ExitShortE	-110	-11	-17	100155	670	0	130	10	120	4
7	AUDUSD	Back101	ChannelCr	Short	0.1M	0.7823	0.7831	16/01/2007 02:00	16/01/2007 08:00	EnterShort	ExitShortC	-80	-8	-14	100086	590	0	120	0	0	7
8	AUDUSD	Back101	ChannelCr	Long	0.1M	0.7836	0.7825	16/01/2007 11:00	16/01/2007 17:00	EnterLong	ExitLongE	-130	-13	-19	99990	460	0	140	140	270	7
9	AUDUSD	Back101	ChannelCr	Long	0.1M	0.7833	0.7827	16/01/2007 21:00	16/01/2007 23:00	EnterLong	ExitLongC	-60	-6	-12	99930	400	0	120	0	0	3
10	AUDUSD	Back101	ChannelCr	Short	0.1M	0.7818	0.7824	17/01/2007 00:00	17/01/2007 01:00	EnterShort	ExitShortC	-60	-6	-12	99870	340	0	90	0	0	2
11	AUDUSD	Back101	ChannelCr	Long	0.1M	0.7831	0.7866	17/01/2007 04:00	18/01/2007 15:00	EnterLong	ExitLongE	350	35	29	100015	690	0	40	570	220	36
12	AUDUSD	Back101	ChannelCr	Short	0.1M	0.7838	0.7724	24/01/2007 03:00	30/01/2007 00:00	EnterShort	ExitShortE	1140	114	108	100555	1830	0	50	1320	180	87

Figure 15.1 The top 13 rows of trades for the AUDUSD backtest

Figure 15.1 shows the top few rows of our spreadsheet with the columns we have been working on highlighted. The account size column can also been formatted as currency if required.

It is now possible to highlight the Account Size column and create a graph with the Excel Chart Wizard. This chart provides a realistic equity curve for the strategy as it includes slippage and money management rules.

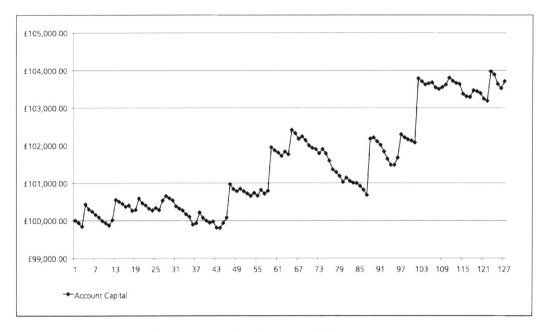

Figure 15.2 Equity curve for AUDUSD using the Channel Crossover strategy

The equity curve in figure 15.2 for our one year, out of sample backtest shows a relatively jagged equity curve with only a modest 4% tax-free return. Performing the same analysis over a larger time period or with a greater number of trades would result in a smoother equity curve.

Further Steps

Further detailed analysis can be performed by collating all of the trade results for each of the instruments in the basket into a single spreadsheet. To do this you need to export the trade results of each instrument into Excel. On export, NinjaTrader opens a new Excel worksheet for each instrument. The trader is then required to manually collate each of the worksheets into a single worksheet. For worksheets with a fairly small number of trades it is fairly easy to manually cut and paste the worksheets together. Once collated into a single worksheet it is necessary to perform the steps detailed in the previous chapter to setup columns for the correct number of points per trade, spread/slippage deduction and position size/account capital. Once all of the formulas and calculations are in place you should select the entire contents of the worksheet and sort the data based on the Entry Time column.

Once the data formatting is complete it is now possible to create an equity curve for the whole basket of instruments for the backtest period by using the graph plotting technique presented in the previous section.

Having plotted the graph further detailed analysis can be performed by:

- Varying the initial capital account size by changing the value in Cell P1.

- Varying the spread/slippage per trade by changing the value in Cell O2.

- Varying the percentage risk per trade by modifying the formula in Cell P2.

If you modify the latter two remember to copy the formula down for all the remaining cells in the respective column.

It is also possible to modify the position size by changing the value used for the MAE in Cell P2, but this may invalidate your test results as the original trades were based on the original value and not the modified MAE.

Figure 15.3 shows a smooth equity curve trading from an initial account size of £20,000 with a 1% risk per trade and a MAE of 183 points. The net result is a profit greater than 25%.

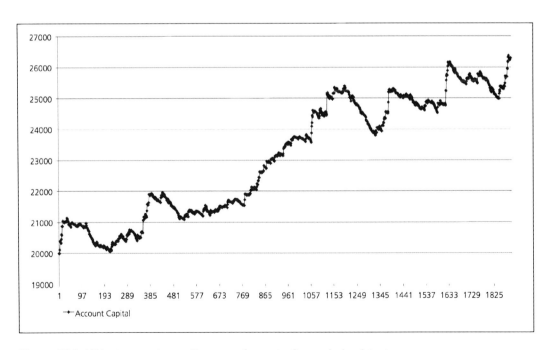

Figure 15.3 All instruments equity curve for out of sample backtest

Additional performance analysis and comparisons against other investments such as bonds, cash savings accounts, ISAs (FTSE 100 index tracker) etc, should be performed, remembering that you get taxed on some investments. Also, the interest rates can vary over the year period so adjust your calculations for this (or take the average value and use that).

16

Real-Time Strategy Testing

Introduction

Real-time testing gives the trader the chance to evaluate their trading system under live conditions but without putting any capital at risk. The real-time testing environment should mirror the live trading environment as closely as possible.

We will cover detail on performing full automation in a later chapter. Without full automation we will have to assume that the trades will be entered manually. Therefore, some notification mechanism from the trading system and the ability to enter, monitor and close positions will be required.

In an earlier chapter we covered different example scenarios for an independent trader setup. In practice the scenarios will vary greatly depending on the traders lifestyle and the markets they trade. In this chapter we will assume that:

- The trader is home based with easy system access both to the trading system, and web access to the spread betting application.

- The trader is trading forex with the Channel Crossover strategy developed in a previous chapter.

- All trades will be placed with a demo spread bet account opened with the spread betting company that the trader's real account is with.

> The demo accounts are usually limited on the real-time prices and the instruments that can be traded.

Real time testing of a strategy has two main functions:

1. To perform further checking that the strategy can be profitable during real-time conditions.

2. To ensure that the strategy is actually tradable. For example, if the system generates several trading signals every few minutes or hours, and you cannot keep up with manually managing these positions, then the strategy may well be profitable but it is likely to be "untradeable" by you.

Figure 16.1 shows a high-level flowchart of the cyclic process followed when system trading a strategy for spread betting.

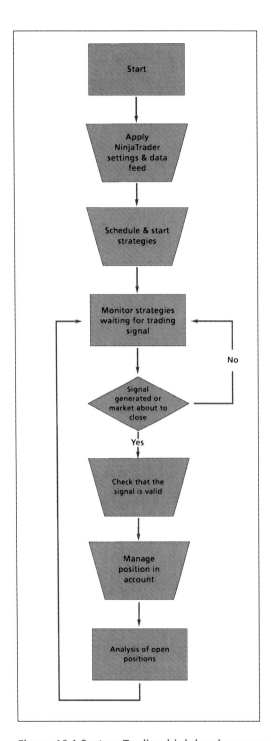

Figure 16.1 System Trading high level process

Step 1. Apply NinjaTrader settings & data feed. This task requires that any pre-trading settings are set before starting the strategy. This includes:

- Waiting until flat before the strategy opens a position.

- Enabling or disabling forex sub-pip.

- Ensuring that the correct data feed or feeds are established.

Step 2. Schedule & start strategies. Start the strategies against the correct instruments and time period with the correct parameters.

Step 3. Monitor strategies waiting for a trading signal. The trading signals will be generated by the strategy automatically and will be documented in the Log tab of Control Centre. At the same time an audible message will be heard. The positions tab shows the open positions.

Step 4. Signal generated or market about to close. If a trading signal has been generated, ie, the opening or closing of a position, then proceed onto the next step. If the market is about to close, and your strategy dictates that you close all of your positions before market close, NinjaTrader will also generate close signals for any open positions. When auto trading NinjaTrader will close positions out approximately 30 seconds before close, however, as you are managing the trades manually for spread betting it may be necessary to close the positions earlier (perhaps five minutes before market close) to give you enough time.

Step 5. Check that the signal is valid. As we are still in the strategy testing phase now is a good time to perform the final check before opening or closing a position to ensure that the trading signal is valid. By valid I mean that the strategy has generated a correct signal based on your trading formula.

If the signal is valid, then proceed on to the next step. If the signal is invalid you should make a note of why you believe the signal to be incorrect. A good practice is also to take a screenshot of the chart at this point so that you can refer back to it during the further analysis phase.

Step 6. Manage position in account. If the signal is valid you are now required to mirror the signal in your spread betting account. For example, if your strategy generated a signal to go long on GBPUSD with a 50-point stop-loss, you should create the same position. When opening the trade you will notice that the prices quoted by the spread betting company are different to your data feed. As discussed in earlier chapters this is a likely situation. Just place the trade anyway! Many spread betting accounts also create an automatic log of positions opened and closed. If yours does not, now is a good time to create a manual record of your trade so that you can compare the NinjaTrading performance results with your actual results at a later time. Also, if you have any problems managing the position, for example the spread betting application is running slowly, or you get requoted, you should make a note of these for future reference.

Step 7. Analysis of open positions. Both open and closed positions should be analysed on a regular basis to ensure that the positions open in NinjaTrader correspond to the positions you have open in your spread betting account. In between actively managing your positions you should also analyse:

- Where have any problems occurred?

- Were any trades not filled by NinjaTrader or the spread betting application?

- Were you unable to take a trade for some reason?

- What is a realistic figure for slippage?

Knowledge of these areas will be essential when you perform detailed analysis of your strategy to ensure that it is profitable and tradable.

Strategy Modification

When real-time testing and sitting at the trading workstation, NinjaTrader provides audible alerts that an order has been filled during strategy execution. If the trader is out on the move, or away from the trading workstation then it is possible to configure the strategy to send an email. The NinjaTrader help guide details how to configure the email system. The steps below detail how to modify our Channel Crossover strategy to send an email when entry and exit criteria are met.

Tools -> Edit NinjaScript -> Strategy and select the Channel Crossover strategy

Select Next several times until the Conditions and Actions screen appears. For each of the six actions we previously defined we need to add an action that sends an email.

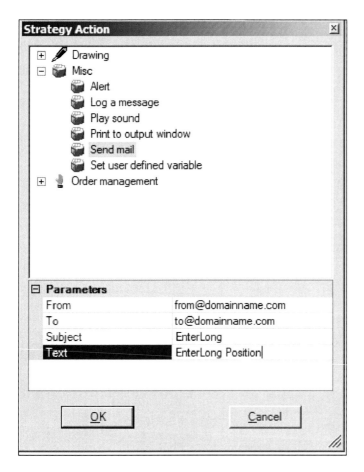

Figure 16.2 Sending an email as an Action

Figure 16.2 shows the Send mail parameters being entered for the resulting email action. The From and To parameters are the Sent From and Send To email addresses respectively and should be set to be email addresses that you have access to.

Unfortunately, in the strategy wizard Send mail option it is not possible to define any text to identify which instrument or strategy has triggered the email. So, if you are currently running multiple strategies and multiple instruments it is impossible to tell which strategy generated the signal.

However, it is possible to do this with the SendMail() function within NinjaScript. Creating NinjaScript applications in C# is outside of the scope of this book, but the NinjaTrader help guide and support forum give excellent guidance on how to achieve this.

Scheduling A Strategy

When scheduling a strategy against an instrument I prefer to use a live chart so that I can see likely trades just before they happen.

Before applying a strategy to run in real-time, I prefer to set the configuration option "wait until flat before executing live". Doing this ensures that a new position is only opened the next time the conditions are met, and prevents a position being opened immediately when the strategy is started.

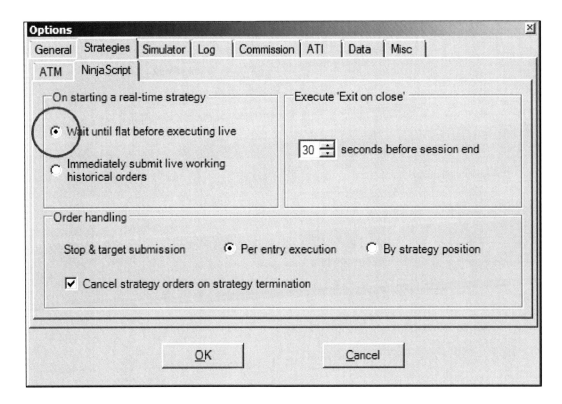

Figure 16.3 Setting wait until flat

Figure 16.3 shows the radio button for Wait Until Flat being selected. The default is to immediately submit live orders. Doing this prevents any historical data causing a new trade to trigger when transitioning from backtesting to live running.

Scheduling a strategy on a chart

The following steps detail how to schedule a strategy using a chart.

Step 1. From NinjaTrader Control Centre select File -> New -> Chart

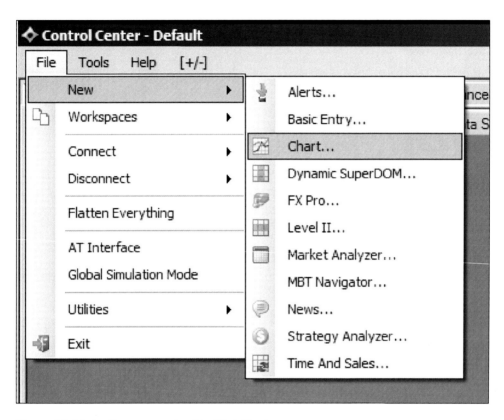

Figure 16.4 Selecting a new chart in NinjaTrader

Step 2. In the Format Data Series window select the chart that you wish to execute a strategy against.

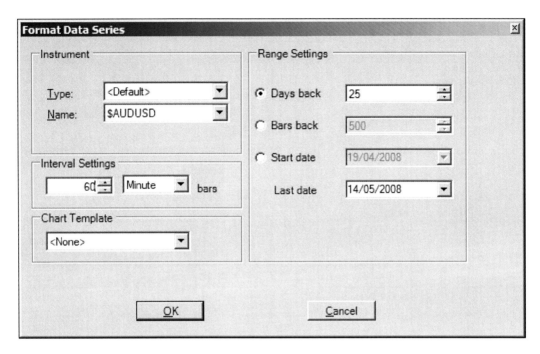

Figure 16.5 Formatting the data series for the chart

For the data series shown in figure 16.5 we have chosen to use AUDUSD on a 60 minute chart because AUDUSD for an hourly time period is one of the instruments we have backtested against.

Step 3. Once the chart is open with the correct instrument and bar period it should be possible to select the strategies button at the top of the chart window as highlighted in figure 16.6.

Figure 16.6 AUDUSD Chart ready to have a strategy applied

Figure 16.7 shows the input parameters, account, exit type and default quantity being selected in the Strategies window. Notice that we will use the default, internal, Sim101 account for testing. If you have any live accounts configured in NinjaTrader be sure not to select them here, otherwise the strategy could trigger real orders.

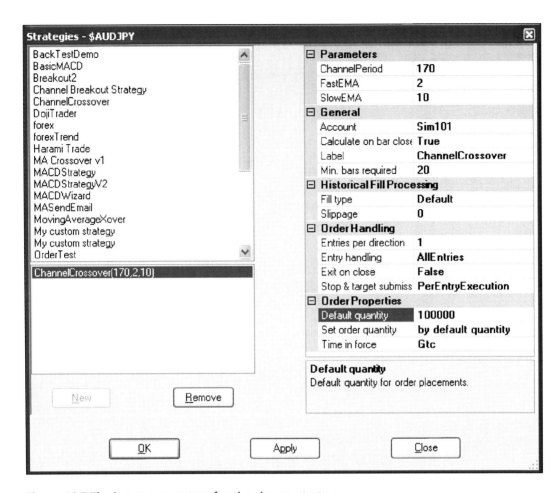

Figure 16.7 The input parameters for the chosen strategy

Once the input strategy parameters have been applied the chart displays the strategy and any plot lines that were set to true during strategy creation. In figure 16.8 we can see that the applied strategy displays our channel and the two moving averages used to close trades.

Figure 16.8 A strategy running against a one hour AUDUSD chart

Position Management

The Channel Crossover strategy that we have scheduled is running on an hourly chart with CalculateOnBarClose set to True. Doing this means that we will only receive trading signals on the hour, and hence only need to check the strategy on the hour. This is great if you are trading a market that is only open during normal daytime hours, but can cause problems if you are trading a 24 hour market such as forex. In this case you will need to work out what you would like to happen should a trade signal be generated during the middle of the night. Some options include:

- Ignore the signal, and hope that the trade was not going to be a big winner! Doing this may have serious consequences for your strategy, and will probably make your backtest results invalid.

- For open positions, it would be possible to tighten up the stop or add a temporary profit target for the overnight period, and perhaps remove them in the morning if the trade is still open.

- Only schedule your strategy to run during daytime hours, and close out any open positions before stopping the strategy at the end of the day.

Opening a position

NinjaTrader will notify the trader when a position is opened. As the strategy is running against the simulated (sim101) account, the position is automatically opened in NinjaTrader, an audible alert occurs, and the trade details can be seen in the Positions and Log tabs.

When this notification occurs it is necessary to manually open the same position with your chosen spread betting company through their trading interface.

Inevitably, some slippage will occur – some favourable, some not – and the prices of NinjaTrader and the spread betting company will not be exactly the same. This difference is also due to the prices quoted by the spread betting company including the spread, and as such the prices are only indicative of the underlying instrument.

If you have a strategy that runs on daily bars then your trade notifications will occur on bar close, which is just as the market closes for the day. You could set the exit time of the strategy to be 15 minutes before the exchange closes, and hence receive any trade notifications on this new bar close. The extra 15 minutes will give you time to place your trades just before the markets close rather than after they open the following day.

Closing a position

NinjaTrader also notifies the trader to close a position with an audible alert and details in the log. The simulated trade is automatically closed and removed from the Positions tab.

The position with the spread betting company should now be closed manually. As before, expect some slippage to occur depending on the volatility of the instrument, and the time taken to actually close the position.

Managing stops and targets

If your system has a clear stop and target strategy, ie, the stop or target is fixed at X points from entry, it is easy to set these values when entering the trade with the spread betting company.

Trailing a stop is more difficult to do. Certainly, trailing a stop point-by-point (unless this feature is supported automatically by the spread betting company) is impractical, or almost impossible to do unless the trader is prepared to manually do this position management. Simplifying a trailing stop strategy, perhaps trailing every five points, or moving to break-even after being X points in profit, is a much more manageable technique.

It is important that you match the stop and target strategy used with the spread betting company to be the same strategy that was used for backtesting. The NinjaTrader wizard only supports a simple stop or trailing stop. However, complex stop strategies can be created in NinjaScript.

Real-time Testing Alternative

Performing at least one month of real-time testing is invaluable for checking the tradability of your strategy. But what happens if your strategy only generates infrequent trades, perhaps only once per month, or once every few months?

NinjaTrader offers an alternative to real-time testing called Market Replay. Market Replay allows the trader to record real-time data, and then replay the data against a strategy at different speeds. For example, several months of data could be replayed in an hour, thus checking a strategy tick for tick, but without the lag of real-time.

17

Real-Time Strategy Execution

System Setup

Having followed the previous testing phases you should now have confidence in your trading system, and be happy to apply its trading signals. The outcome of the real-time testing phase should be that you have created a tradable system that fits in with your lifestyle, and allows you to easily manage the positions when required.

If at this stage you do not have confidence that your strategy is profitable, or you are uncomfortable with the time/effort commitment to manage the positions, then you need to re-address your strategy before proceeding. This is likely to involve re-work on the strategy, perhaps using a different time frame, such as daily charts rather than hourly. This allows you to manage each of your positions just once per day. The obvious side effect of this is that you will get fewer signals, and will possibly have to greatly increase any stop sizes to take into account the daily price swings.

Trading The Signals

A trading system is supposed to remove some of the psychology behind trading, but without the luxury of full automation you are still required to place the trades manually. It would be very easy to slip into the practice of missing a few signals that you think are not profitable and just picking and choosing the ones you think you want to trade. Unfortunately this is not the way to trade a mechanical trading strategy, unless you are totally confident in your ability and have justifiably good reasons not to take the trade. If you deviate from the strategy you run the risk of missing the one big winning trade that boosts your profits or keeps your account alive.

My personal opinion is that if you put in the hard work to develop and test a profitable trading system you should have confidence in the system's ability, and can take the trades it provides with confidence.

The process for trading the system real-time, rather than real-time testing, are identical. The only additional steps that I frequently perform are:

1. A fortnightly calculation of the correlations, and then choose which instruments to trade depending on the correlation metrics.

2. A daily calculation of position size for each trade based on my money management rules and account size. When I trade a large number of strategies that generate frequent trading signals simultaneously, rather than calculate the position size for every trade based on account size, I just calculate the position size once at the start of the trading day and use that position size for all of the day's trades.

3. At the end of each trading day I run a report in NinjaTrader to obtain the current performance metrics of the strategies and account. These metrics will not be exactly the same as the actual metrics in the spread betting account, but they will be similar. I compare this report with the actual figures in my spread betting account.

18

Full Automation

Switch It On And Walk Away…

Up until this point we have discussed trading systems that require the opening, closing and management of positions to be performed manually. Depending on your strategy time frame, this might not pose a problem as you may only be trading on end of day data. However if your strategy runs on a 15 minute time frame, and uses forex, the requirement to open and close positions on a regular basis or in the middle of the night exists.

Full automation is the opening and closing of positions by the strategy itself, requiring no manual intervention. The reason why we have not discussed full automation until this chapter is because at the time I started writing this book only a single spread bet company offers full automated trading. This company is called Futuresbetting.com

Preparation For Auto Trading

Before setting up a full automated trading system, these high level items are required:

- A trading system, including money management strategy that you have thoroughly tested and are confident to trade.

- A software license for NinjaTrader.

- A funded account with a broker that allows automated trading and that the NinjaTrader software can connect to.

- A computer connected to the Internet that you can leave switched on for the entire duration that the strategy is running.

NinjaTrader is free for system development, testing and running against the simulated account. To enable a live connection to a broker, a license is required. NinjaTrader offer a range of license options to suit trading styles and budget.

Once a license has been purchased, a brokerage account is required. The account details are configured as an account connection within NinjaTrader. The NinjaTrader help manual has detailed instructions for creating an account connection to most brokers once the username and password have been obtained.

For details of NinjaTrader supported brokers, other than Futuresbetting.com please refer to the NinjaTrader website. The real account will also need to be funded. Some of the non-spread-betting companies such as MBTrading offer demo accounts. The demo accounts come with a nominal amount of simulated funds. If using a demo account initially try to set the capital size to be roughly what you will actually trade with when funding a real account.

I personally do not run my live strategies from the same workstation that I develop and test systems on. I have a separate server that I leave running. From experience I have also found it beneficial to have multiple instances on NinjaTrader running, one for each broker connection. I do this by using VMWare Workstation to have several virtual workstations running on the same PC hardware. I do this so that if I encounter any software problems, or have to modify a strategy, or if I experience any connectivity issues with an individual broker, then these issues are generally isolated to a single trading workstation and do not affect the others.

Running A Strategy

Running a trading strategy for automated trading follows the same process used to run a strategy covered in previous chapters. With NinjaTrader two approaches exist:

- Run the strategy from a chart.

- Run the strategy from the Strategies tab in Control Centre.

Running the strategy from an open chart has the benefit that it is possible to see the instrument's price action, and by also knowing the underlying formula for the strategy you are able to determine if a position is near to being opened/closed.

The disadvantage of running the strategy from a chart is that you need to open a chart with the correct time period for each instrument, and then select the strategy, and then enter all of the strategies parameters. This can become tedious if you have a strategy running for multiple instruments at the same time and regularly wish to stop and restart the strategy.

Before attempting to schedule a strategy ensure that you have a live connection to the required broker. In figure 18.1, the bottom left hand corner of the NinjaTrader Control Centre shows active connections.

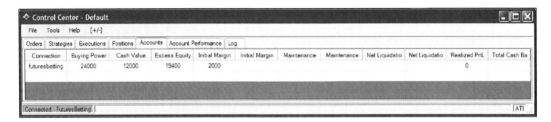

Figure 18.1 A current connection to Futuresbetting.com

The Log tab within control centre also has further details of the connection.

Scheduling a strategy from the Strategies tab

Scheduling a strategy from the strategies tab only requires the trader to right click on the main window of the strategies tab within Control Centre and select New Strategy. A New Strategy window appears using the same input format used when backtesting. In addition to the parameters selected previously, the trader is required to select a time series. Selecting OK when complete displays the strategy and its parameters. At this point the strategy is not running. The trader must select the Start button on the right hand side.

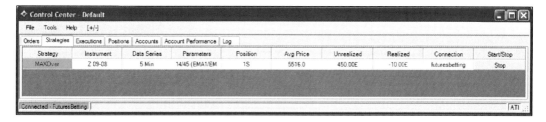

Figure 18.2 A strategy running in the strategies tab for a single instrument

The strategies tab also details any open positions running against the strategy. In figure 18.2 we can see the following:

- The Moving Average Crossover (MAXOver) strategy is being used.

- The strategy has been applied to the FTSE 100 09-08 Futures contract on a five minute chart with the parameters 14 (EMA1) and 45 (EMA2).

- A single short position is open, currently in profit by £450.

- A previous trade has taken place, with a loss of £10.

- The strategy name is highlighted in green which indicates that the strategy is running.

What Does Go Wrong

My personal view of using full automation with a system trading strategy is that to some extent you can walk away from the system and allow it to run in the background untouched. I believe that the trader should feel liberated from their trading workstation (and should not feel that they need to watch the strategy on a continuous basis) on condition that the system developer:

- Has spent enough time developing and testing the strategy.

- Is comfortable with how the strategy performs in various markets.

- Has adequate system stops or system safety features built in.

But (and there is always a but) things can go wrong, and occasionally they do. In this section I have documented all of the things that have gone wrong whilst I have been auto-trading an account.

Microsoft Windows update

As discussed in the platform setup section, my trading platform is running on Microsoft Windows. As the server has a permanent connection to the Internet, it is obviously a good idea to ensure that the system is regularly updated with Microsoft security and firewall software patches. Unfortunately I had not realised that some of the Windows updates require the server to be rebooted. If you have not scheduled the automatic updates correctly, Windows tends to perform this reboot whenever it feels like it. This causes a problem during the middle of a trading session. I have since modified the Windows update process to download the updates when they become available, but not to apply the patches during trading hours.

Broker's server down for maintenance

All of the brokers I have used for auto trading perform regular maintenance on their servers. Should the server require a long period of downtime, the broker nearly always notifies any account holders with an advance warning. Shorter periods of downtime, usually around five minutes, tend to happen on a daily basis. When this downtime occurs, NinjaTrader reports that it has lost connection to the broker and trading is ceased. The downtime is usually scheduled for the middle of the night or very early in the morning when either the markets are closed, or in the case of forex trading, little market activity occurs. The problem I have found is that sometimes after the broker has finished maintenance the connection between the auto-trading application and the brokers server is not automatically restored, and some manual human intervention is required to re-establish the link.

Loss of Internet connection or power cut

With a residential broadband connection and power supply in use by the independent trader, losing either of these utilities always causes concern. Where I currently live both of these tend to occur on a regular basis. In order to minimise the risk from both of these I always place a stop when entering a position with the broker. In addition, I also have a laptop with a 3G data card and my trading software installed to allow access to the broker's system to manually manage the open positions until my residential broadband and/or power is restored.

Trading software and trading account out of sync

Many of the brokers providing real-time API connections to NinjaTrader have two-way communication in place allowing NinjaTrader and the broker instant updates of positions and prices. Some connections, such as the connection to Collective2, only occur in a single direction. For example, when NinjaTrader is running against a Collective2 account and sends a trade signal the communication is unidirectional, and NinjaTrader is unaware of whether the information was received by the Collective2 servers. Occasionally this allows NinjaTrader and the Collective2 account to get out of synchronisation. NinjaTrader shows an open position, yet the corresponding open position does not show on Collective2.

The first time this happened to me I made the mistake of trying to close the open position in NinjaTrader. For example, in order to close an open long position for ten contracts, NinjaTrader would create a sell order for ten contracts. Unfortunately, as Collective2 did not have an open long order for ten contracts, when it received the sell order, it actually opened a short position for ten contracts, but closed the position in NinjaTrader. I was able to flatten (and sync) the account by entering a manual trade on the Collective2 website, but not before the sell order had gone well out of the money, and my Collective2 account had taken a loss of almost 10%.

Market goes crazy

Occasionally the market does go crazy. When this happens open trades tend to go to extremes, either hitting the stops or running up a massive profit. This tends to cause problems with strategies based on higher time frames with no stops in place. For example, if your strategy is set to perform calculations on bar close on an hourly chart and the market goes crazy within an hour period, with no stop in place you could suffer large losses before the hour period is up and your strategy closes the trade.

Also, if the market is rapidly changing between extreme high and low prices the strategy may suffer greatly from whipsaws during this period.

Strategy goes wrong or stops running

I cannot emphasise enough how important strategy testing really is. This does not just mean ensuring that your strategy is profitable and the performance metrics are healthy, but also confirming that all of the trade signals are generated correctly. On several occasions I have created a strategy that performs well and the metrics look good. I have then set the strategy running against an account and noticed something small that I could tweak, made the small change, but accidentally affected something else. I have learnt to minimise these mistakes, but make sure that you document any changes you make, and ensure that you backtest the strategy again, no matter how small you perceive the change to be.

Other problems include scheduling a strategy against the wrong instrument by accident, and entering too many zeros when setting the position size. The current version of NinjaTrader does not have the ability to bulk schedule a single strategy against multiple instruments, so each strategy has to be manually scheduled. During this repetitive process I have found it very easy (to my financial cost) to rush and end up with a few typographical errors with the parameters and position sizes.

Occasionally due to a programmatic error in the strategy, or a software bug, the strategy or trading application will terminate. Sometimes your open positions will be closed at this point, and sometimes they stay open when the strategy stops running.

Appendix – Further Strategy Examples

Example Strategy – Inside Bar Breakout

An inside bar is defined as a bar where the range has been contained within the prior bar's trading range. In this example the current bar's high and low do not exceed the previous bar's high and low.

When two or more sequential inside bars occur, a volatility play can be implemented. The more inside bars that occur, the greater the chance a surge of volatility, or breakout, could occur. Usually, an inside bar breakout is actually developed as an inside day breakout, and daily bar data is used. For this example strategy, the time periods used are six hour bars, giving us four defined time periods per day, roughly corresponding to the different global market opening times.

Strategy formula

Long Entry

Identify a currency pair where the two previous six hour bars have been contained within the prior bar's range.

Buy when the current bar close is higher than the previous three bars.

Short Entry

Identify a currency pair where the two previous six hour bars have been contained within the prior bar's range.

Sell when the current bar close is lower than the previous three bars.

Position Exit

Exit the position on a trailing stop.

Condition	Position Trigger	Formula
1	Open Long	If High[2] < High[3] and
		If Low[2] > Low[3] and
		If High[1] < High[2] and
		If Low[1] > Low[2] and
		Close[0] > High[3]
2	Open Short	If High[2] < High[3] and
		If Low[2] > Low[3] and
		If High[1] < High[2] and
		If Low[1] > Low[2] and
		Close[0] < Low[3]
3	Close Position	Trailing Stop

Table 19.1 Formula used for inside bar strategy

Strategy creation

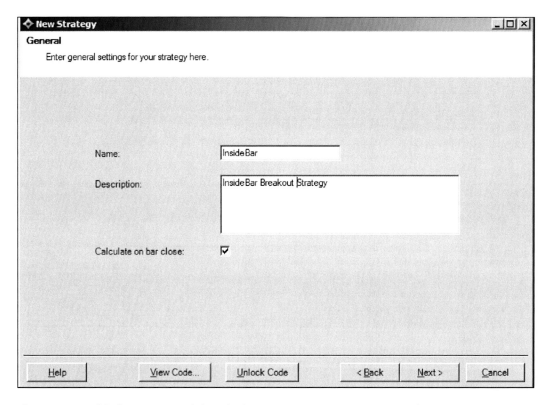

Figure 19.1 Inside bar name and description

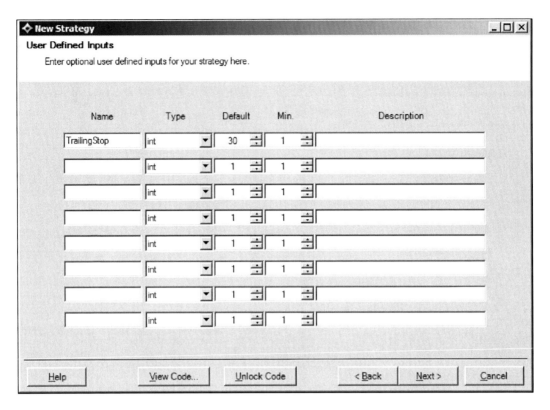

Figure 19.2 Inside bar parameters

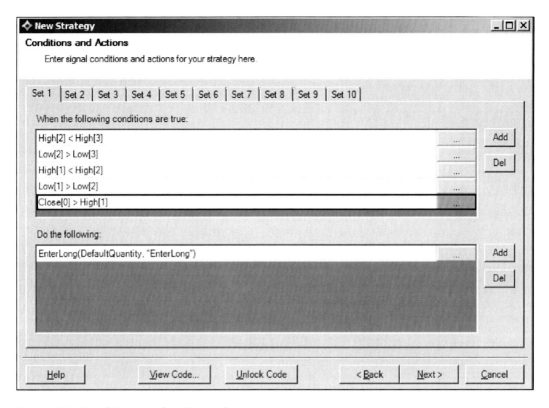

Figure 19.3 Conditions and Actions tab 1

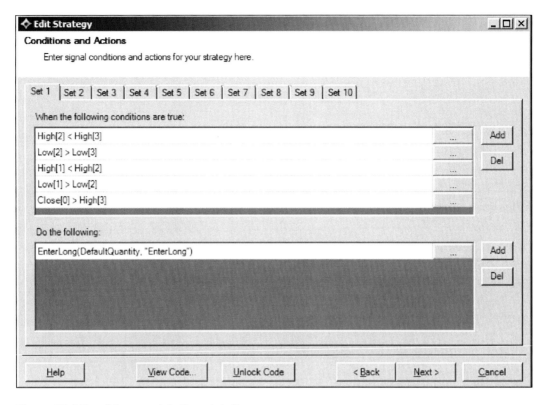

Figure 19.4 Conditions and Actions tab 2

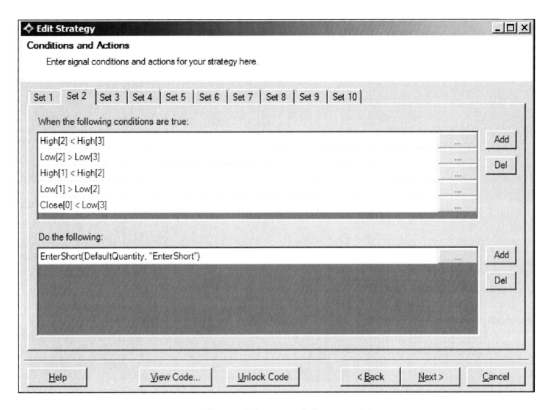

Figure 19.5 Setting a trailing stop for both long and short positions

Inside bar, initial backtest

Results for 6 hour chart for GBPUSD 1/1/2004 to 1/1/2007:

Instrument	Trailing Stop	Total Net Profit	Profit Factor	Max. Drawdown	Sharpe Ratio	Percent Profitable	Average MAE
GBPUSD	100	-3,560	0.76	-3.56%	-0.11	25.71%	0.30%

Table 19.2 Inside bar, initial backtest results

The initial backtest results shown in table 19.2 are not profitable. On closer examination of the trades, it is possible to see that:

• Only using a trailing stop to close the position is preventing some of our winning trades maximising their profit.

- We also seem to miss a large part of the breakout waiting for confirmation (ie, close[0] > high[1]). In real-time trading we could obviously open the position as soon as the breakout occurs and not wait for the current bar to close, however we cannot backtest this using the static data. In addition, if we were trading real time, we could also set the stop to be just below the low price for the previous bar (bar[1]).

Inside bar strategy modifications: part 1

Rather than waiting for confirmation of the breakout, and potentially missing much of the breakout gains, the strategy has been modified to check for the inside bar conditions, but then open a position based on the current price in relation to a medium period simple moving average. This is because we could expect the price action to break out and return back to the moving average.

- Open a long position if price action below the SMA

- Open a short position if price action above the SMA.

- Exit the position when the price reaches the SMA.

Condition	Position Trigger	Formula
1	Open Long	If High[2] < High[3] and
		If Low[2] > Low[3] and
		If High[1] < High[2] and
		If Low[1] > Low[2] and
		Close[1] < SMA[0]
2	Open Short	If High[2] < High[3] and
		If Low[2] > Low[3] and
		If High[1] < High[2] and
		If Low[1] > Low[2] and
		Close[1] > SMA[0]
3	Close Long	High[0] >= SMA[0]
4	Close Short	Low[0] <= SMA[0]
5	Close Position	Trailing Stop

Table 19.3 Modified formula for the inside bar strategy

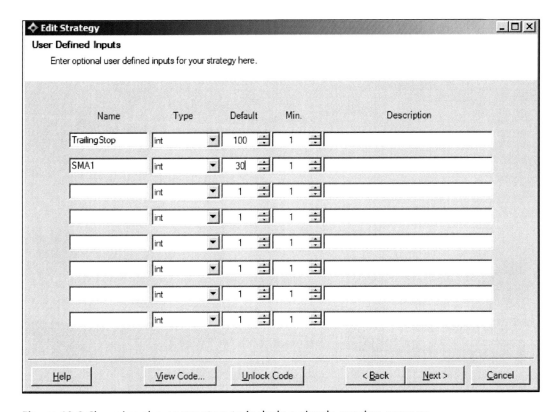

Figure 19.6 Changing the parameters to include a simple moving average

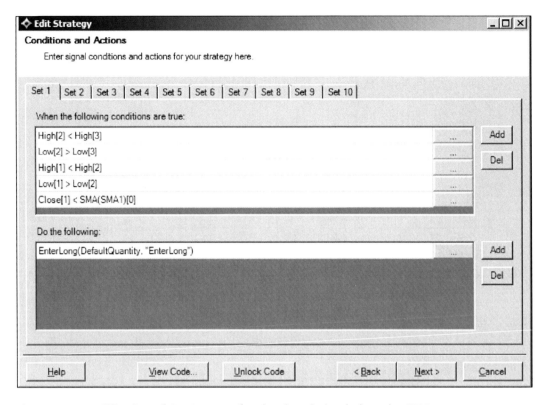

Figure 19.7 Modification of Set 1 to test for the close being below the SMA

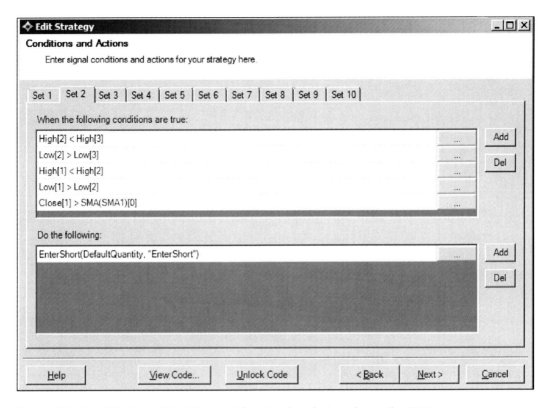

Figure 19.8 Modification of Set 2 to test for the close being above the SMA

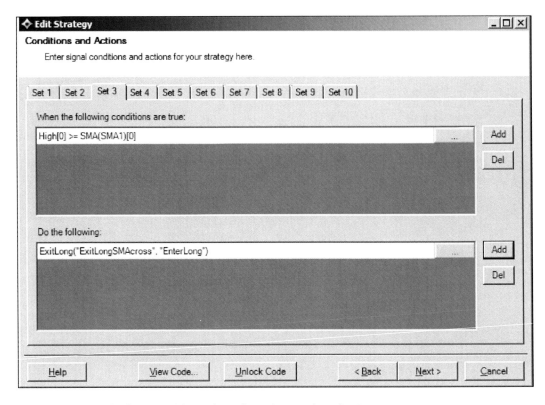

Figure 19.9 Exit the long position when the price reaches the SMA

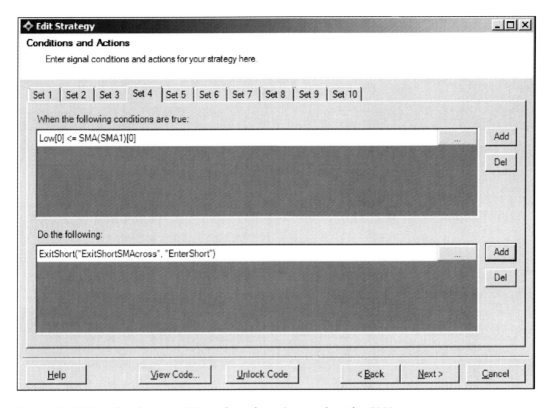

Figure 19.10 Exit the short position when the price reaches the SMA

Inside bar, second backtest

Results for the six hour chart for GBPUSD between 1 January 2004 and 1 January 2007.

When performing the earlier backtest it was apparent that the trailing stop was having too much impact on the trades, so the stop value was placed much further out.

Instrument	SMA	TrailingStop	Total Net Profit	Profit Factor	Max. Drawdown	Sharpe Ratio	Percent Profitable	Average MAE
GBPUSD	30	200	4,520	1.11	-3.50%	0.07	63.16%	0.42%

Table 19.4 Backtest results for modified inside bar strategy

Strategy modifications: part 2

For this round of strategy modifications we have re-introduced the directional breakout bar back into the formula. Ie, perform a confirmation check on the breakout bar before opening a position, but rather than looking for a breakout higher than all three of the previous bars, we are only concerned with the price breaking above the most recent bar. As previously discussed, waiting for this confirmation will reduce our profit when backtested against static data. In real-time testing/trading we could change the strategy so that as soon as the price breaks out the position could be opened. Also, we have removed the trailing stop in favour of a static stop-loss.

Condition	Position Trigger	Formula
1	Open Long	If High[2] < High[3] and
		If Low[2] > Low[3] and
		If High[1] < High[2] and
		If Low[1] > Low[2] and
		Close[1] < SMA[0]
		Close[0] > Close[1]
2	Open Short	If High[2] < High[3] and
		If Low[2] > Low[3] and
		If High[1] < High[2] and
		If Low[1] > Low[2] and
		Close[1] > SMA[0]
		Close[0] < Close[1]
3	Close Long	High[0] >= SMA[0]
4	Close Short	Low[0] <= SMA[0]

Table 19.5 Modifications to inside bar formula

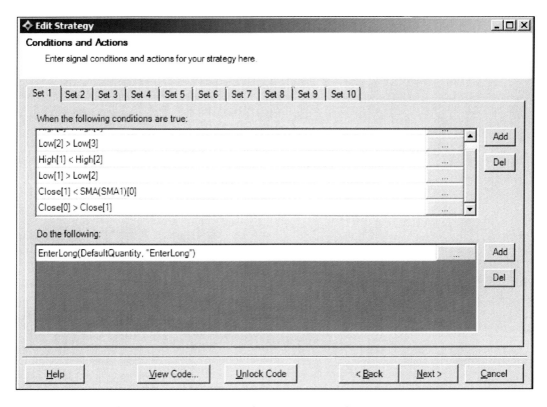

Figure 19.11 Modification of Set 1 to wait for breakout confirmation

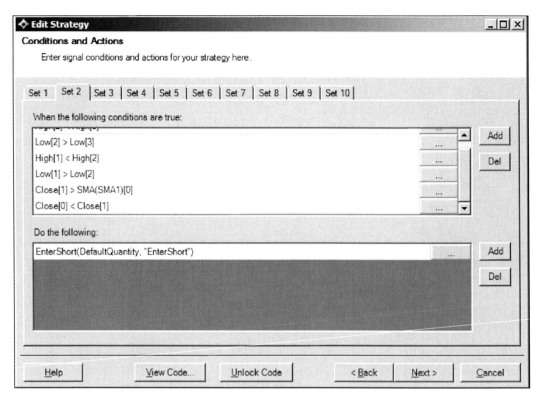

Figure 19.12 Modification of Set 2 to wait for breakout confirmation

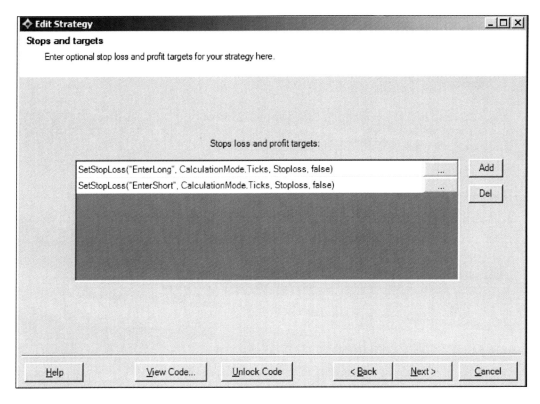

Figure 19.13 Changed to use static stop value rather than trailing stop

Inside bar, third backtest

Results for the six hour chart for GBPUSD between 1 January 2004 and 1 January 2007.

Instrument	SMA	Stop-loss	Total Net Profit	Profit Factor	Max. Drawdown	Sharpe Ratio	Percent Profitable	Average MAE
GBPUSD	30	100	3,540	1.16	-2.02%	0.08	60.32%	0.30%

Table 19.6 Backtest results for modified inside bar strategy

Inside bar optimisation

We will now use the optimisation feature of NinjaTrader to curve fit a series of successful parameters for our strategy to our basket of instruments.

In the Strategy Analyzer window, select the Optimise button.

Change the parameters and time frame as per table 19.7.

Parameter	Range	Step
Stop-loss	100 – 200	50
SMA1	30-50	5
Time Frame	1/1/2004 to 1/1/2007	n/a

Table 19.7 Optimisation parameter ranges and step

Instrument	SMA1	Stop-loss	Total Net Profit	Profit Factor	Max. Drawdown	Sharpe Ratio	Percent Profitable	Average MAE
AUDUSD	50	150	-3,230	0.86	-12.44%	-0.03	66.67%	0.92%
CHFJPY	50	200	3,340	1.25	-3.99%	0.04	62.50%	0.80%
EURCHF	50	200	6,990	1.63	-1.56%	0.19	62.77%	0.29%
EURGBP	30	150	950	1.09	-4.01%	0.04	57.89%	0.53%
EURJPY	35	100	5,510	1.2	-4.26%	0.08	59.52%	0.44%
EURUSD	35	100	-8,810	0.78	-12.26%	-0.11	53.66%	0.49%
GBPUSD	30	200	18,360	1.46	-4.32%	0.16	69.50%	0.42%
NZDUSD	30	100	-2,310	0.82	-9.60%	-0.04	64.47%	0.67%
USDCAD	35	200	5,870	1.17	-4.42%	0.06	62.04%	0.52%
USDCHF	35	150	-3,490	0.95	-10.44%	-0.03	57.96%	0.53%
USDJPY	40	100	6,340	1.24	-2.62%	0.09	62.63%	0.42%

Table 19.8 Optimised parameters

Inside bar, out of sample backtest

Using the parameters at either end of our ranges (30 and 200 for SMA and Stop-loss respectively) on an out of sample date range provides the results shown in table 19.9.

Parameter	Range
Stop-loss	200
SMA1	30
Time Frame	1/1/2007 to 1/1/2008

Table 19.9 Out of sample parameters

Instrument	Total Net Profit	Profit Factor	Max. Drawdown	Sharpe Ratio	Percent Profitable	Average MAE
AUDUSD	1,270	3.08	-0.48%	0.25	62.50%	0.49%
CHFJPY	2,440	2.64	-1.52%	0.18	70.00%	0.50%
EURCHF	-3,690	0.3	-2.53%	-0.29	50.00%	0.44%
EURGBP	1,100	2.2	-0.71%	0.32	45.45%	0.55%
EURJPY	2,560	1.51	-1.45%	0.13	66.67%	0.44%
EURUSD	-260	0.96	-3.05%	-0.03	52.63%	0.45%
GBPUSD	6,580	5.39	-0.40%	0.77	75.00%	0.28%
NZDUSD	900	1.6	-1.21%	0.13	60.00%	0.84%
USDCAD	4,770	2.48	-1.99%	0.41	68.42%	0.56%
USDCHF	370	1.08	-1.58%	0.02	54.17%	0.48%
USDJPY	5,500	6.61	-0.64%	0.36	77.78%	0.40%

Table 19.10 Out of sample results for basket of instruments

Inside bar, detailed results analysis

Exporting all of the trades into a single file for detailed analysis, and sort them by EntryTime gives the equity curve displayed in figure 19.14.

Due to the strategy using a large stop-loss of 200 points, and only risking 1% of account capital per trade, this strategy needs to be traded from a large starting capital to allow a sufficient position size unless the trader wishes to allow a higher degree of risk per trade, in which case a smaller account capital can be used.

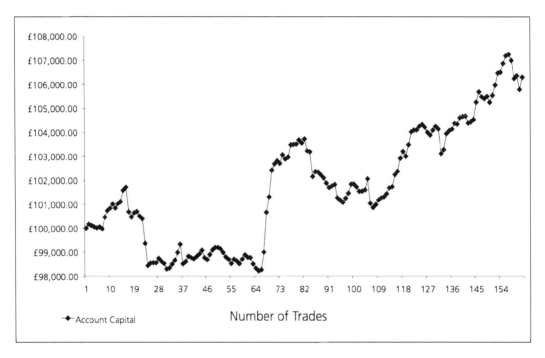

Figure 19.14 Equity curve obtained by exporting all of the trades into a single file and then sorting by EntryTime

Using a smaller starting capital of £10,000, but taking on a larger percentage of risk of 5% of account capital per trade, provides the equity curve shown in figure 19.15.

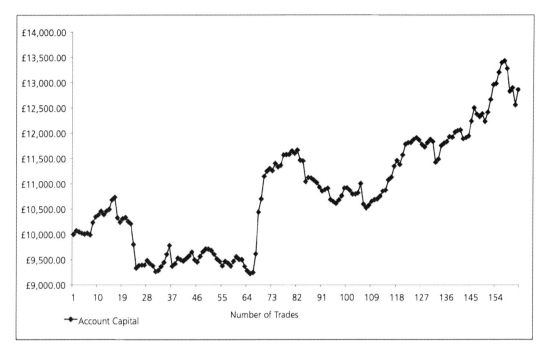

Figure 19.15 Equity curve obtained by taking a smaller starting capital of £10,000, and taking on a larger risk at 5% of account capital

Example strategy – perfect order

A moving average perfect order strategy is a trend following strategy that requires several moving averages of different bar periods to be in sequential order. Figure 19.16 shows an example short trade in a downtrend. It is possible to see that:

- SMA(10 Period) is less than SMA(20 Period)
- SMA(20 Period) is less than SMA(50 Period)
- SMA(50 Period) is less than SMA(100 Period)
- SMA(100 Period) is less than SMA(200 Period)

In an uptrend, for a long trade, the order would be reversed.

Figure 19.16 A perfect order short trade

The perfect order is a strong indicator of momentum on the side of the trend.

Strategy formula

Long entry

Enter a long position when the perfect order occurs for all five moving averages in a bull trend.

Short entry

Enter a short position when the perfect order occurs for all five moving averages in a bear trend.

Position exit

Close the position as soon as the perfect order no longer exists. In practice this will be when the two fastest moving averages – SMA(10) and SMA(20) – cross.

Condition	Position Trigger	Formula
1	Open Long	SMA1 > SMA2 and
		SMA2 > SMA3 and
		SMA3 > SMA4 and
		SMA4 > SMA5
2	Open Short	SMA1 < SMA2 and
		SMA2 < SMA3 and
		SMA3 < SMA4 and
		SMA4 < SMA5
3	Close Long	SMA1 crosses below SMA2
4	Close Short	SMA1 crosses above SMA2

Table 19.11 Perfect order formula

Strategy creation

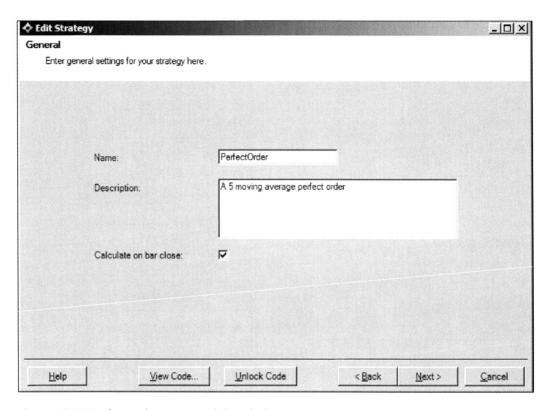

Figure 19.17 Perfect order name and description

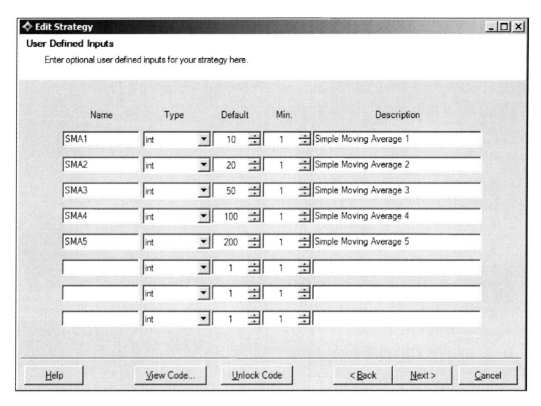

Figure 19.18 Perfect order parameters

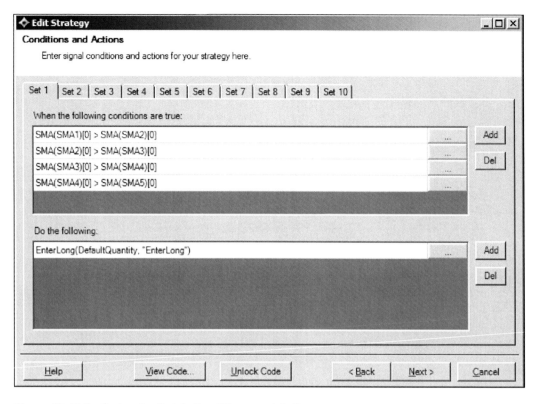

Figure 19.19 Perfect order Set 1: Conditions and Actions

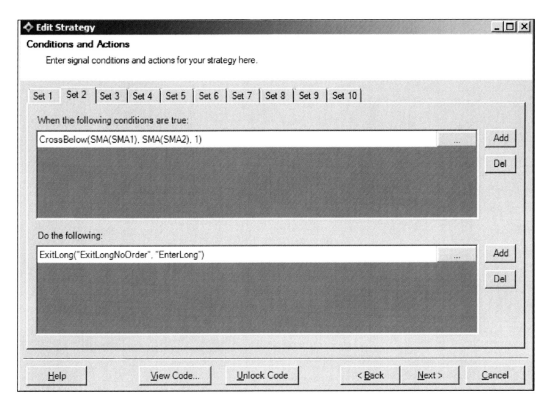

Figure 19.20 Perfect order Set 2: Conditions and Actions

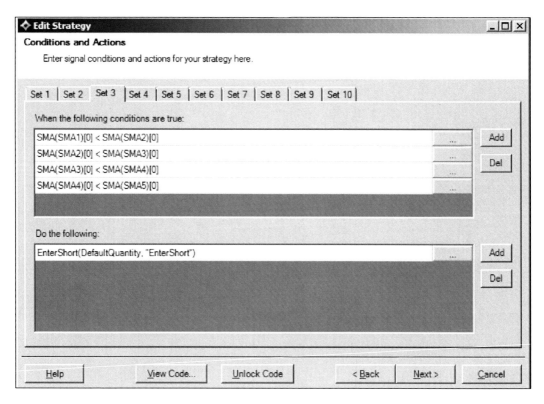

Figure 19.21 Perfect order Set 3: Conditions and Actions

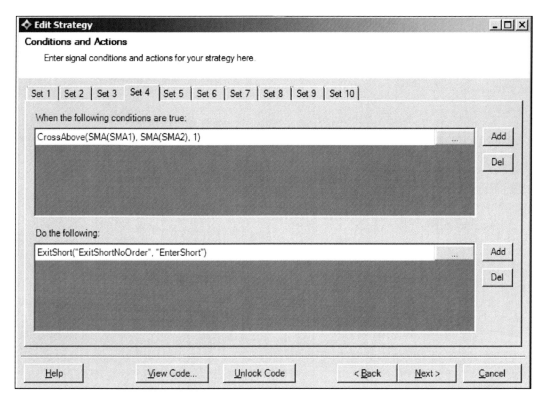

Figure 19.22 Perfect order Set 4: Conditions and Actions

Perfect order initial backtest

Initial backtest to prove correct functioning of strategy using GBPUSD between 1 January 2006 and 1 January 2007.

Instrument	Parameters	Total Net Profit	Profit Factor	Max. Drawdown	Sharpe Ratio	Percent Profitable	Average MAE
GBPUSD	10,20,50,100,200	3,020	1.11	-4.22%	0.1	35.64%	0.26%

Table 19.12 Perfect order initial backtest

Figure 19.23 shows the strategy triggering two short trades when the moving averages form sequentially. It is possible to see that the two shortest period moving averages briefly touch/cross which triggers the first trade to close, but then as the price action moves lower the perfect order is formed once again and a second short trade is opened.

Figure 19.23 Two short trades when the perfect order forms

Figure 19.24 shows a long perfect order trade.

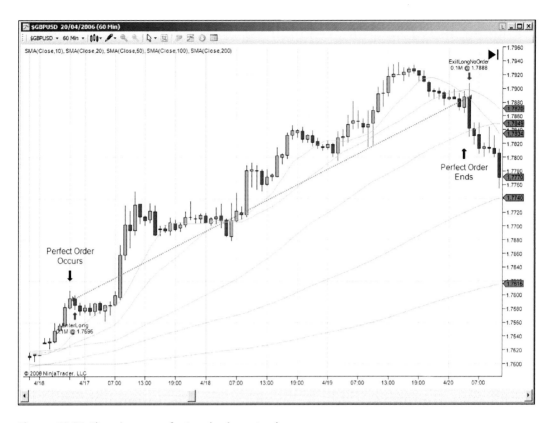

Figure 19.24 Showing a perfect order long trade

Perfect order optimisation

We will now use the optimisation feature of NinjaTrader to essential curve fit a series of successful parameters for our strategy just against GBPUSD.

In the Strategy Analyzer window, select the Optimise button.

Change the parameters and time frame as shown in table 19.13 and optimise based on profit factor. Be aware that with this many parameters, if you decided to optimise against the entire basket of instruments, the optimisation process will take several hours.

Parameter	Range	Step
SMA1	5 – 15	1
SMA2	16 – 32	2
SMA3	35 – 65	5
SMA4	70 – 130	10
SMA5	140 – 260	20
Time Frame	1/1/2004 to 1/1/2007	n/a
Bar Period	60 minute bars	n/a

Table 19.13 Optimisation parameters for the perfect order strategy

Instrument	Optimised Parameters	Total Net Profit	Profit Factor	Max. Drawdown	Sharpe Ratio	Percent Profitable	Average MAE
GBPUSD	15,26,35,120,240	26,250	1.37	-2.73%	0.41	38.62%	0.30%

Table 19.14 Results of optimisation

Instrument	Optimised Parameters	Total Net Profit	Profit Factor	Max. Drawdown	Sharpe Ratio	Percent Profitable	Average MAE
GBPUSD	15,26,35,120,240	-1,570	0.95	1.57%	-0.10	35.16%	0.28%

Table 19.15 Out of sample backtest for data between 1 January 2007 and 1 January 2008

The out of sample results listed in table 19.15 show that our previously optimised parameters have failed to produce a profitable return for the out of sample period. The reason for this could be that the perfect order strategy just did not work well during 2007. Maybe the GBPUSD instrument did not experience many long running trends. Another, more probable reason is that we have over-optimised the parameters, and essentially curve fitted the strategy to the price data. This is a common problem when having a relatively large number of parameters for a strategy and trying to perform an extensive optimisation.

One option to overcome this problem is to limit the number of parameter variations. This can be achieved by increasing the step values during the optimisation process and repeating the optimisation using the whole basket of instruments.

Parameter	Range	Step
SMA1	6 – 14	2
SMA2	16 – 32	4
SMA3	35 – 65	10
SMA4	70 – 130	20
SMA5	140 – 260	40
Time Frame	1/1/2004 to 1/1/2007	n/a
Bar Period	60 minute bars	n/a

Table 19.16 Optimisation parameters with an increased step size

Instrument	Optimised Parameters	Total Net Profit	Profit Factor	Max. Drawdown	Sharpe Ratio	Percent Profitable	Average MAE
AUDUSD	6/32/35/70/260	10,360	1.45	-5.18%	0.3	44.13%	0.34%
CHFJPY	14/28/45/70/180	-3,080	0.9	-8.18%	-0.08	43.20%	0.39%
EURCHF	12/32/35/130/180	1,910	1.14	-1.18%	0.09	38.85%	0.16%
EURGBP	8/28/35/70/140	2,540	1.2	-4.44%	0.13	42.62%	0.23%
EURJPY	10/20/35/130/260	2,850	1.08	-6.42%	0.06	46.89%	0.30%
EURUSD	6/28/65/110/140	13,000	1.33	-3.80%	0.26	36.76%	0.31%
GBPUSD	14/28/45/130/260	22,540	1.46	-3.07%	0.36	41.22%	0.33%
NZDUSD	14/32/65/70/260	6,900	1.26	-7.15%	0.18	43.75%	0.48%
USDCAD	10/32/35/70/220	-8,430	0.8	-7.15%	-0.21	40.46%	0.36%
USDCHF	10/28/55/130/140	9,180	1.22	-3.42%	0.17	37.99%	0.36%
USDJPY	6/16/55/110/220	12,230	1.45	-4.59%	0.31	38.83%	0.25%

Table 19.17 Results of optimisation with increased step size

Calculating the mean, median and mode of the optimised parameters produces the results in table 19.18.

Statistic	SMA1	SMA2	SMA3	SMA4	SMA5
Mean	10	28	45	99	205
Median	10	28	45	110	220
Mode	6	28	35	70	260

Table 19.18 Three sets of optimised parameters

Without going into detailed analysis for each of the three sets of optimised parameters, just using the mode values and performing an out of sample backtest for the entire basket of instruments produces the results in table 19.19. It is clear to see that these results are more favourable than the results produced by our overly optimised, or curve fitted, parameters from the previous example.

Instrument	Total Net Profit	Profit Factor	Max. Drawdown	Sharpe Ratio	Percent Profitable	Average MAE
AUDUSD	-3,110	0.86	-8.49%	-0.13	33.33%	0.39%
CHFJPY	450	1.04	-4.12%	0.02	39.29%	0.27%
EURCHF	1,980	1.18	-2.67%	0.15	35.00%	0.14%
EURGBP	110	1.02	-3.01%	0.01	41.98%	0.17%
EURJPY	8,480	1.36	-3.56%	0.27	40.00%	0.88%
EURUSD	2,830	1.18	-2.55%	0.2	37.50%	0.20%
GBPUSD	4,800	1.23	-2.16%	0.25	36.05%	0.22%
NZDUSD	6,750	1.4	-6.35%	0.39	39.56%	0.85%
USDCAD	3,190	1.2	-3.67%	0.18	32.32%	0.28%
USDCHF	-4,050	0.79	-7.89%	-0.22	28.72%	0.27%
USDJPY	3,640	1.21	-4.35%	0.26	32.14%	0.31%

Table 19.19 Out of sample backtest results using parameters (6,28,35,70,260)

Conclusion

This strategy example has demonstrated that it is possible to over optimise a set of input parameters to curve fit the strategy against the available data. Once this has been performed, the strategy is unlikely to produce such favourable results on out of sample data and during real-time execution.

Future enhancements for this strategy could include the use of ADX to provide confirmation that the instrument is trending before a position is opened.

Glossary

3G

Third Generation of mobile phone technology. 3G usually refers to a data connection provided by a network operator.

ADSL

Asymmetric Digital Subscriber Line. A data communications technology that enables fast data transmission over copper telephone lines.

ASCII

A standard of character encoding based on the English alphabet.

Broker

A party that mediates between a buyer and a seller.

Curve fitting

The process of strategy over-optimisation to produce the best returns from a financial instrument for a given time period.

DAX

Deutscher Aktien Index. A stock market index consisting of the 30 major German companies.

Drawdown

Unrealised or realised losses from a trading account.

EBIT

Earnings Before Interest and Taxes

EFS

eSignal Formula Script. A programming language used by the eSignal charting package.

Forex

Foreign Exchange market exists wherever one currency is traded for another.

FTSE

FTSE Group is a UK provider of stock market indices. The letters FTSE are no longer an abbreviation.

GPRS

General Packet Radio Service. Sometimes called 2.5G. A low rate mobile data transfer service.

HMRC

Her Majesty's Revenue and Customs. UK tax regulator.

Instrument

Various types of financial transactions.

Latency

A time delay between something being initiated and the moment the first effect begins.

NASDAQ

One of the American stock exchanges.

OHLC

Open, High, Low, Close. The four prices available from a candlestick or bar chart.

OTC

Over The Counter. Trading by broker-dealers in instruments not listed or traded on any exchange.

P/E ratio

Price/Earnings ratio. A measure of earnings multiple.

P&L

Profit and Loss. An income statement.

Portfolio

A collection of investments held by an institution or a private individual.

Position

An open financial trade, either long or short.

SATA

Serial Advanced Technology Attachment. A computer bus designed for data transfer between a computer and a storage device.

Wizard

A tool to enable the simplification of a process.

Index

O

offer price 12

office space 18

OHLC prices 21, 24, 66, 73, 258

Olsen Financial Technologies 24

open, high, low and close prices, see 'OHLC'

open if touched 14

optimisation, see 'strategy'

order types 14

OTC, see 'over the counter'

out of sample

    backtest 188

    data 126-128

over the counter (OTC) products 13, 75, 258

overnight interest 15

P

P/E ratio 65, 259

percentage profitable 131, 185, 188

performance metrics 129-137, 187, 212

pivot points 66

player accounts 11

portfolio 259

    diversification 34-35

position

    close 9, 10, 14

    definition 259

exit 222, 243

management 208-210

    tools 14, 16

open 4, 10, 14-15, 209

    simultaneous 54

size 4, 11, 15, 212

sizing 48-54

    fixed 49

    per point 50-53

triggers 222, 228, 234, 243

positive progressive systems 47

power cuts 217

price movement 66

prices 12-13

probability 2

processing delay 13

profit & loss accounts 40, 259

profit factor 132, 185

profit targets 14, 19

    exits 88-90

progressive betting 47-48

Pryor, Malcolm vii

psychology 5-6, 59

R

ranging period 94

real-time

    data 13, 17, 21-22, 29, 32

        delayed 21

V

Venn diagrams 36

VMWare Workstation 214

Vodafone 33

volatility 14, 32

W

Wait until flat 203

whipsaws 94, 123, 151, 188-189, 218

why trade? 5-6

wifi 19

Wizard 259